SUCCESSFUL LIVING ROOMS

Project Ideas and Instructions to
Build a Bar, Entertainment Center,
Conversation Pit, Accent Wall, Fireplaces

Jay W. Hedden

Structures Publishing Co.
Farmington, Mich. 48024

Manufactured in the United States of America

Edited by Shirley M. Horowitz

Cover photo courtesy of Hedrich-Blessing; Chicago, Ill. Designed by Architects Frazier, Orr, Fairbanks, and Quam; Geneva, Ill.

Cover design by Richard Kinney

Book design by Carey Ferchland, Typographic Insight, Ltd.

Current Printing (last digit)
10   9   8   7   6   5   4   3   2

Structures Publishing Co.
Farmington, Mich. 48024

Library of Congress Cataloging in Publication Data

Hedden, Jay W.
    Successful living rooms.

    Includes index.
    1. Dwellings—Remodeling.   2. Living rooms.
I. Title
TH4816.H43   643'.7   77-26025
ISBN 0-912336-60-9
ISBN 0-912336-7 pbk.

SUCCESSFUL LIVING ROOMS

CONTENTS

With thanks to Monte Burch, whose assistance resulted in a much better book.

Introduction

Have you ever sighed enviously over some beautiful living room—and wished that you could cheaply, easily transform your own? Wouldn't you like a free-standing or built-in bar—or a bay window that opens your living room to a lovely view? Could your living room use dramatic lighting or an impressive fireplace, perhaps with a raised hearth and wood storage?

Most people do not realize that they can create relaxing atmospheres, party moods, and good times in their living rooms with either their own carpentry skills or imaginative use of prebuilt component parts for entertainment centers, storage walls and dividers, entertainment bars, sunken living rooms or conversation pits, and many other stunning and exciting living room features.

This book brings together ideas, plans and products, designs and recommendations that will help you choose and then carry out the desired project. Step-by-step instructions, photos and diagrams, and knowledgeable tips ensure not only a practical and inexpensive addition to your living room, but a professional-looking one as well.

If you start with a well defined plan—and you should—you can do the work in stages, as time and money permit. The room will be usable until you start the next stage of remodeling, and you just might find some new ideas you'd like to incorporate as you go along.

Getting What You Want

Why change your present living room? Because a modern living room is no longer an old-fashioned parlor that is used only when company comes. A living room should be *lived in*.

Yes, you might want the room to be just for quiet relaxing and reading, perhaps listening to music. Or maybe you want a room that's designed for entertaining, with a bar and an entertainment center. Then you can build a bar, and a place for the stereo components. You might want the components on open shelves for an informal look and atmosphere, or perhaps you'd prefer to have them hidden away when they are not used. The bar can be a fixed piece of furniture, or it too can be hidden when not in use.

A living room can be a "multipurpose room." On one evening it might hold a free-and-easy party with drinks, another night it could be for listening to music—hard rock or the classics or the "big band sound." Just design the room so it can change personalities with just a few adjustments.

If you don't want everything on open shelves, how about a paneled wall a foot from an existing wall? Doors can be cut into the paneling and "Tutch-Latches" installed so no knobs or pulls show. You push to open and push to close. An attractive paneled wall, but with hundreds of cubic feet of storage accessible at the push of your hand.

Lighting is important; if you want a subdued light for quiet listening to classical music, you can install a dimmer switch in place of a regular switch. This is a job anyone can do, if he or she can turn a screwdriver and knows where to shut off the electricity to the circuit that powers the switch.

Will you want a fireplace? Free-standing units can be installed almost anywhere, but be sure you can run the chimney up to the roof. This may not be a problem in a one-story house, but in a two-story dwelling you'll have to figure on running the chimney up through a closet, then the attic and through the roof. Which means you'll lose closet space, and others in the family might take a dim view of that kind of arrangement.

If it's just the look of a fireplace you want, you can build a realistic-looking one that has electric logs. They'll glow and flicker just like real flames, but the fire can be stopped and started with the flip of a switch.

Why not consider turning your living room into a "Great Room," which many new houses now feature —with a small living room nearby. In this case you definitely will want a fireplace. Flooring can be of several types, even carpeting, but it's not recommended when there's the chance of spilled beverages and dropped cigarettes. Instead, you'll want vinyl flooring in square tiles or sheet material, or perhaps even ceramic tile. Modern adhesives make installing ceramic tile a genuine do-it-yourself job and the hard surface is ideal for dancing and there is practically nothing that can damage it.

Planning Ahead

Even if you don't do the work yourself, having a comprehensive plan of what you want will save both time and money. You can explain to the contractor exactly what is involved in the job, and he then can give a close estimate of the time and cost involved. As with any job, of course, get two or more estimates, and look at the "bottom line." What might sound like a low bid could be the highest, when the contractor's finance or other special costs are added to that bid.

Splitting the Work Load

One cost-saving arrangement is for you to handle everything but major structural changes.

A professional contractor can do the installation of a bay, larger window, or sliding glass door in a day, and you then can do the painting or other finishing as your time allows, with the room closed in weathertight.

A really experienced do-it-yourselfer could even handle these major jobs, but in most cases a building permit would be required. If you can't prove that you can handle such a job without risking damage or weakening the structure, getting the permit might be difficult.

Small-scale furniture makes tiny living room seem larger. Light-colored expanse of carpet, installed in squares, also gives a more spacious impression. (Photo courtesy of Armstrong Cork Co.)

1. Planning and the Basics

To start your room remodeling, you first must decide what kind of a room you want. Then sit down with pencil and paper and make a sketch of the room to scale. This can be done on ¼-inch-square graph paper, using a scale of ¼-inch square equals 1 foot. Some critical dimensions, however, must be shown to $^1/_{16}$-inch for accuracy. Measure the room carefully and mark in each door and window. Note where there are wall plugs (receptacles). Unless you are going to tear open a wall so you can relocate the receptacles, it's best to design your remodeling so they are accessible. Be careful in your measurements: you want to know exactly how wide the room is and how long. How far are windows and doors from the adjacent walls? Walk around the room and examine it with a critical eye. Can any of the doors be eliminated to provide more wall space? Closing in a door is a fairly simple job, well within the capabilities of any handy do-it-yourself home owner.

Are you going to have different furniture, or perhaps built-ins? Carefully draw these on your plan. Draw and redraw until you are absolutely certain that the floor plan is what you want. It is a lot less work and expense to change lines on a drawing than to make structural changes after you start.

Look at your traffic pattern. Can people walk into and out of the room without stumbling over furniture or climbing over tables? This may sound like a basic consideration, but think of some of the living rooms you have been in recently. It's very possible the furniture was arranged so there was only a one-person path into and out of the room, and you had to wait your turn to enter and leave. This is not conducive to a friendly get-together.

Electrical Requirements

If the living room is going to be an entertainment center, check for electrical outlets that will be needed for stereo components, television sets, electric organs and other devices that require electric power.

If your home has been built within the last few years, there probably will be plenty of wall outlets, as the Na-

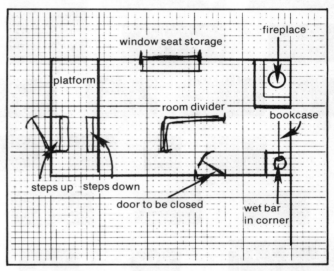

Graph paper permits quick and accurate scale drawing. Each of the outlined squares is ¼ inch, which represents 1 foot in the full-size room. Measure the furniture you are going to use—or built-ins you plan to construct—and carefully draw them on the plan.

tional Electric Code (NEC) requires outlets spaced no more than 6 feet apart, horizontally, on every wall. If your home is older, there probably will not be an adequate number of outlets.

Even in a newer home, your personal requirements may dictate more receptacles than present, with some much closer than the Code requirement of 6 feet. Furniture may be placed in front of some receptacles, or construction of a built-in may require relocation of an existing receptacle.

Also make sure that the room has more than one circuit from the electrical service box. This assures that should a fuse blow or a circuit breaker kick out and some lights go out, there will be lights on the other circuit to permit you to find your way out of the room to replace the fuse or reset the breaker.

Adding new receptacles is not a difficult job if you are going to panel a room, as you can cut a groove in the existing plaster or plasterboard and run the wires in it,

Cut-Out Templates

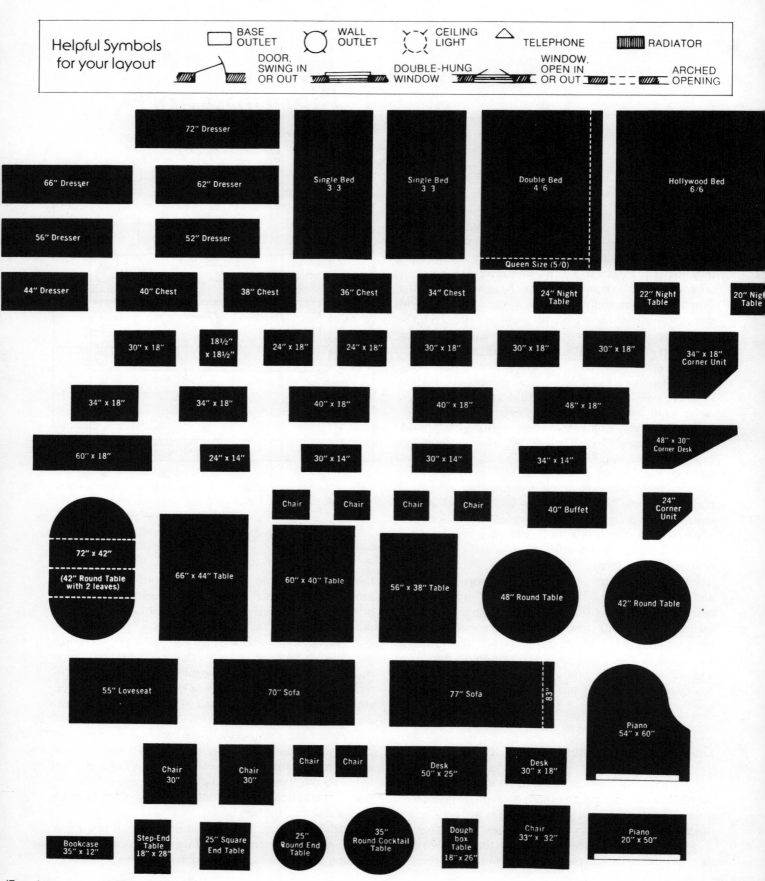

Helpful Symbols for your layout

BASE OUTLET | WALL OUTLET | CEILING LIGHT | TELEPHONE | RADIATOR

DOOR, SWING IN OR OUT | DOUBLE-HUNG WINDOW | WINDOW, OPEN IN OR OUT | ARCHED OPENING

72" Dresser

66" Dresser | 62" Dresser | Single Bed 3/3 | Single Bed 3/3 | Double Bed 4/6 | Hollywood Bed 6/6

56" Dresser | 52" Dresser

Queen Size (5/0)

44" Dresser | 40" Chest | 38" Chest | 36" Chest | 34" Chest | 24" Night Table | 22" Night Table | 20" Night Table

30" x 18" | 18½" x 18½" | 24" x 18" | 24" x 18" | 30" x 18" | 30" x 18" | 30" x 18" | 34" x 18" Corner Unit

34" x 18" | 34" x 18" | 40" x 18" | 40" x 18" | 48" x 18"

48" x 30" Corner Desk

60" x 18" | 24" x 14" | 30" x 14" | 30" x 14" | 34" x 14"

24" Corner Unit

Chair | Chair | Chair | Chair | 40" Buffet

72" x 42"

(42" Round Table with 2 leaves) | 66" x 44" Table | 60" x 40" Table | 56" x 38" Table | 48" Round Table | 42" Round Table

55" Loveseat | 70" Sofa | 77" Sofa | 83" | Piano 54" x 60"

Chair 30" | Chair 30" | Chair | Chair | Desk 50" x 25" | Desk 30" x 18"

Bookcase 35" x 12" | Step-End Table 18" x 28" | 25" Square End Table | 25" Round End Table | 35" Round Cocktail Table | Dough box Table 18" x 26" | Chair 33" x 32" | Piano 20" x 50"

(Templates courtesy of Ethan Allen, Inc.)

Scale: ¼ in. equals 1 ft.

When you are talking basics in a room, consider making changes that require the least amount of work. You can spend a lot of time tearing out a wall, when it might be just as useful to simply open the wall and fit in shelves, leaving the basic structure intact.

Add a Bar?

If the living room is to be more than an entertainment center for music lovers, you might want to add a bar. If it's to be a wet bar, then you'll have to think of plumbing and drains. Both hot and cold water can be run in pipes of rigid or flexible plastic, which are easy to connect to the existing water lines, and easy to route up through floors and walls.

Drains also can be plastic pipe, but finding a drain connection close to where you want to locate the bar may be a problem. Drains must slope down away from the sink after they are routed down through the floor. A fairly large drain pipe slanted down across the basement will really be in the way which gets us back to that basic planning. Locate a drain in the basement, then figure where in the living room you can conveniently locate a bar. It might be handy in one corner of the room, or on one of the walls. There is no reason why it cannot be free-standing somewhere in the room, acting as a room divider. With a few thoughts as to its design, it can look like a cabinet when it's not being used as a bar, and not at all out of place when the room is used as a living room rather than a place for serving beverages.

There also is no reason why the bar cannot be in an adjacent room, with a pass-through and bar counter in the wall. The opening can be closed off when you wish by either hinged doors at the side, or a drop-down door that is pivoted up out of the way and hooked to the wall. If there is no convenient drain line under the living room, or even water lines, locating the bar in the adjacent room might be the only solution.

If it's to be a "dry" bar, the same idea can be used to create a bar that doubles as a breakfast or snack bar. This is ideal if the kitchen is adjacent to the living room.

Is the living room next to a closed-in porch? Decorate the porch to match the decor of the living room, so that the porch extends the living room, and adds a touch of the outdoors. The porch might also be a good location for a bar.

Insulating

Screens on the porch will bring in the fresh air in summer, but in the winter you'd better figure on insulat-

Where it's not possible to tear open a wall for added wiring, surface-mounted plastic raceways for wiring can be used. The raceways screw to the wall, have snap-on covers. Receptacles can be located where you want them. The plastic covers can be painted to match or contrast with the wall. (Photo courtesy Carlon)

stapling it at the intersection of the wall studs. Receptacle boxes can be fitted in holes cut in the wallboard and nailed to a stud. If you are not going to panel, one method of running the wire is to first remove the baseboard and make a groove behind it for the wire. After the wire is installed, the baseboard is replaced. Be sure to mark the location of any wires, so you do not nail through them when you apply paneling or replace the baseboard.

Structural Decisions

While you are evaluating the room for changes, consider the removal of any "stub" walls between the living room and a dining or other adjacent room. These short walls were once in vogue; some will have bookcases or shelves in the lower portion, while others will simply be blank walls.

You may not want to remove these stub walls completely, but you can open them up by removing the plaster or wallboard, then paneling part of them—with a double 2 x 4 or a 4 x 4 post to replace the removed 2 x 4 studs—and leaving the lower portion for shelves or a cabinet.

Ceramic tile, here quarry tile, creates firm smooth surface that wears practically forever, is easy to clean. This porch, adjacent to living room, is decorated to be an extension of the living room. Wrought-iron furniture carries out casual-living theme. (Photo courtesy Tile Council of America)

ing glass to keep in the heat. Insulation in the floor, ceiling and walls will help too. If you can't quite afford insulating glass for the porch (or living room), by all means install a storm sash. This will reduce heat loss through the windows by about 50 percent.

Taking Stock of Problems and Solutions

When you actually start the remodeling job, if at all possible, clear the room of all furnishings. This means furniture, carpets, pictures on the wall, everything. You now have a "clean piece of paper" on which to create the room you want. A room empty of furnishings very often looks completely different than when it was filled with things with which you have been familiar for years.

Walls

Examine the walls carefully. Is the plaster or plasterboard on the outside wall, or walls, in poor condition? Would it be a good idea to remove the old wall cover and replace it with new? Now is the time, and if your house needs insulation, you can do it at the same time and make your house more energy-efficient. We'll get into the actual step-by-step of this in the chapter on "Structural Changes." That chapter also will cover closing in an unused door and other projects that require actual changes to the basic structure of the room, or house.

With the room empty, now is the time to paint the walls and ceiling, if you are going to do that in your redecorating. Do you want to set off one end or corner of the room to be a special area? A wainscoting might be what you need. Paint the wall (or paper it) down to about 3 feet above the floor, then apply the wainscoting. This can be purchased in a "kit" that includes the short lengths of paneling and the trim molding for the upper edges. It is applied to the wall with panel adhesive and a few nails. Full instructions for the installation are included in the kit. (See end of Chapter 9.)

Floors

Look over the floor. Is it in rather poor condition? If it's hardwood, consider renting a floor sander and sanding off the old finish and applying a new one.

Would you rather have carpeting? You will definitely if the floor is ordinary plywood, which is the case with many homes built in recent years. You can apply do-it-yourself carpeting in two ways; carpet squares or full-width material that comes in 6 and 12-foot widths. The squares can be applied with special carpet adhesive, or you can buy the squares of carpeting with a self-adhesive. A paper back is peeled off the carpet and it is simply pressed down on the floor. The adhesive does not set up immediately, but firms up over a day or so as it is walked

Paneling on wall has been applied horizontally instead of vertically, as commonly done. Paneling also is used to cover built-in seat, shelves and simple table supported at one end by wall, at other by wooden post. Note lights on ceiling beam that pivot in all directions for special effects. (Photo courtesy Azrock Floor Products.)

If you plan to install carpeting or flooring, it will be easier if you first empty the room of all furnishings. Instructions for applying carpet squares or resilient tiles will give first step as finding the exact center of the room and drawing lines that intersect at right angles. (Photo courtesy Armstrong Cork Co.)

Decor of this living room is definitely Victorian, with wicker and rattan furniture. Window that has no view is covered with trellis purchased at a lumberyard. Trellis projects above window to form "cornice" to which drapes are attached. (Photo courtesy Wall Covering Information Bureau)

It's not always possible to clear a room when you want to install flooring, so it must be done by moving furniture around as you do the job. Carpet squares are fairly easy to apply in these circumstances, but sheet flooring or carpeting would present major problems. (Photo courtesy Armstrong Cork Co.)

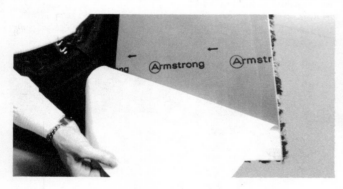

Carpet tiles like these require only peeling off backing paper to permit applying to any clean, dry surface. A cushion is "built right in" to the carpet squares, so no padding is required. (Photo courtesy Armstrong Cork Co.)

To fit a carpet square around pipe or other obstruction, make paper pattern 12 x 12 inches, then trace it onto back of carpet square, cut to fit with sharp scissors. (Photo courtesy Armstrong Cork Co.)

To cut and fit carpet squares next to walls, place a loose square on top of last full square in any row—this applies also to vinyl or other resilient tiles—and make sure pattern or arrow is properly aligned. Over this tile or square that is upside down, place one right side up, butted against the wall. Use last tile to mark along first one, then cut to fit. (Photo courtesy Armstrong Cork Co.)

on by you and the family. Which means you can adjust and move any squares that do not quite fit properly.

In a room with many projections or corners, or where there are columns or exposed pipes, the squares are the easiest to install, as they are easily trimmed to fit in these areas. If the room is fairly clear of any problems, then the full-width carpeting will be the easiest. There also will be fewer seams to catch dust and dirt. The carpeting does not require adhesive all over the room, but simply around the perimeter and at doorways. Metal or plastic trim strips are fitted in doorways to protect the carpet edges and prevent it from being kicked loose from the floor.

If the room will be used for entertaining where food and drinks will be involved, carpeting may not appeal to you. Spilled beverages and party dips are a bit difficult to remove from a carpet, but can easily be wiped up from a resilient-flooring material. Here again, you have a choice of squares, or tiles, and sheet material.

The tiles are easily installed one at a time, and they also are available plain, to be applied with troweled or brushed-on adhesive, and with self-adhesive that is exposed by peeling off a paper backing. The sheet material is applied by stapling along the edges, and trimming at doorways with metal or plastic strips.

There is one more kind of flooring that you might consider for at least part of the room, and that is ceramic tile. The floor must be firm and smooth, which might require gluing and nailing down hardboard, particleboard or plywood underlayment. Underlayment generally runs ¼ or ⁵⁄₁₆ inches thick, and covers a floor that is damaged or has cupped and warped boards. It can be used under carpeting and resilient flooring also, where necessary.

Ceramic tile comes in several thicknesses, and in an almost infinite number of colors and patterns. It is applied with a mastic or adhesive, then a grout is brushed into the joints between the tiles when the mastic has set overnight so the volatile vehicle of the mastic has evaporated. Be sure that the grout you use is the type formulated for

If you want the look of parquet flooring without the expense and trouble of real wood, new vinyl tile has such a realistic look it's difficult to tell it from the real thing. Just peel and stick it down. (Photo courtesy Armstrong Cork Co.)

Fitting floor tiles diagonally gives different look to this living room that also is hobby center. Note open shelves, drawers beneath for storage. Woven hangings on either side conceal other open shelves, as well as add southwest desert accent. (Photo courtesy Armstrong Cork Co.)

Sheet vinyl flooring is reproduction of clay tile, cleans easily, and can be installed by the do-it-yourselfer. Here fireplace is in center of one end of living room, "conversation pit" is created by seating arrangement. Note heavy redwood beams that create rugged, rustic look, along with wall paneling. (Photo courtesy Armstrong Cork Co.)

floors, rather than for walls. The floor material is much more resistant to wear and stains.

Any of the flooring materials can be purchased at lumberyards, larger hardware stores and at home centers. This is true of all the materials described in this book. Where a true home center is near you, that's the place to buy what you need, as they will have everything from flooring to paneling to ceiling materials, as well as lumber, plywood, wallcoverings and hardware. It also is true that some lumberyards and hardware stores sell the same wide variety of materials, but don't call themselves by the term "home center."

Ceilings

Ceilings are another area where you can change the character of a room. If you have an older home with high ceilings, which means more space to heat and cool, you can lower the ceiling with one of several kinds of suspended ceiling. This reduces the volume of air to be heated and cooled, and also gives a modern look to the room.

This corner of living room has ceramic tile on the floor to stand up to rough treatment. Tweed furniture and rugged tables also are chosen to withstand boisterous teenagers. Generous storage closet has bifold doors that permit access to all shelves, yet do not project very far into room when opened. (Photo courtesy Tile Council of America)

16

Suspended ceilings have been around for several years; you hang a grid of metal T-shapes and angles from wires, then fit the tile into the resulting framework. Newer systems of suspended ceilings are designed so the metal does not show on the ceiling, but only around the perimeter, on the walls. Even on those ceiling systems where the metal shows, the manufacturers have come up with tile that is designed to minimize the metal, and make it part of the overall pattern.

The variety of patterns available in ceiling tile ranges from very simple to extremely sculptured. If your living room is to be of modern or contemporary decor, the plain tile would be suitable, while the more classical designs would be appropriate if your choice of decor is to feature period furniture and traditional appointments.

In this suspended ceiling the metal support grid shows, but the tile is patterned so the grid is part of that pattern. Tiles are 2 x 4 feet, lift out easily for access to area above ceiling. (Photo courtesy Armstrong Cork Co.)

Unusual wallcovering on both walls and ceiling makes this living room exciting and special. Louvered door closes off adjacent kitchen, but allows ventilation (and music and conversation) to pass through. (Photo courtesy Wall Covering Industry Bureau)

Fireplace is almost a "must" in a Great Room, which your living room can become if you design it that way. Modern prefabricated units that look like masonry units, as this one does, can be installed by a handy home owner. Note glass doors that keep sparks in, prevent loss of heat up the chimney, produce gentle radiant heat. Furniture here is a mix of modern overstuffed, rococo-base coffee table, chrome cube, accented by hanging driftwood, feathers and unusual corner niche. Rather wild wallcovering that goes with the "eclectic" decor shows the kind of fun decorating you can have in a Great Room. (Photo courtesy Birge Wallpaper, "Tatanka" American Indian design wall covering)

The "Great Room"

Another innovation in new homes in recent years is the "Great Room." This is a combination living room, den, family room, recreation room and entertainment area. If there is another living room in this kind of house, it usually is quite small and reserved for the very infrequent formal get-togethers once reserved for the old-fashioned parlor.

You might want your present room to be converted to a great room; this takes a bit more planning—and possibly more time and material.

With only rare exceptions, there is a fireplace, either a conventional masonry unit, or one of the modern pre-fabricated models. Masonry fireplaces require extensive skills, which means it's a job for a professional. Installing one of the many designs of prefabricated fireplaces, however, is definitely a do-it-yourself project, and many such fireplaces are sold on that basis. We will describe such a project in the chapter on fireplaces.

Often a Great Room will have a rustic, informal decor. This will include rustic wall paneling, ceiling beams (real or simulated), sometimes heavy wooden columns that may or may not be genuinely structural, plenty of built-ins and often a lot of windows. In some parts of the country a Great Room is called a "Florida" room, and it originated as a screened-in, glassed-in room on one side of a house in the warmer areas of the country. This quite likely is the reason some Great Rooms have many windows. From the screened-in room, the Florida room evolved into a more closed-in room, with more solid walls, and the other features now found in Great Rooms.

Because a Great Room is devoted to informality, the furnishings reflect this. The decor often is "eclectic," that word that pretty much means "anything goes." Furniture can be a mix of chrome and glass, wrought iron, wicker, upholstered and even some items that look like they are made of slabs of wood or even brick or masonry.

This kind of decor definitely is in the realm of the do-it-yourselfer, and refinished, refurbished second-hand furniture looks right at home.

If you want to change your living room to a Great Room, you will have a lot of fun, and quite possibly will have a room that will change personality over the years as you replace various pieces of furniture with new-found items, or redecorate to suit your mood at a particular time of the year.

Now there's the kind of a living room that's really lived in!

Who Will Do The Job?

This applies to those of you who will "do-it-yourself." Anyone who figures on having a contractor or other professional do the job of remodeling a living room will have him get the necessary material. But it is still up to you, the home owner, to plan the room and determine what kind of a room it will be. No contractor can read your mind or know what you really want unless you can show him a well thought out plan.

A contractor (a good one) can show you where you can minimize time, trouble and expense by making some simple changes, or substituting one material for another. If you do employ a contractor, be sure to get several estimates from different firms. Be sure in all cases to get an estimate on the same plan, with the same materials, fixtures, etc., so the man is making an estimate on the same job, with the same amount of time and materials involved.

There really is no reason, however, than many reasonably handy home owners cannot do the whole job. Manufacturers have spent years of time and millions of dollars to develop materials that a do-it-yourselfer can install. We've had paneling and resilient floor tile for many years, but now we have sheet flooring and carpeting that is designed specifically for installation by the do-it-yourselfer. The big advantage in do-it-yourself is quite simple: cost. The dollar amount for labor on any kind of job runs from three to five times the cost of the material required. Which means that if you need two hundred dollars' worth of paneling to do a room, a contractor will charge from six hundred to one thousand dollars. In this day and age, that's a lot of money you can save for yourself. Or use to buy other materials or furniture.

2. Structural Changes

Before you start making structural changes in your living room, you must know the difference between a "load-bearing wall" and a "non-load-bearing wall."

First, all exterior walls are load-bearing walls, unless your home is of "post-and-beam" construction. In this type of construction the outer walls consist of heavy 4 x 4, 4 x 6 or even heavier vertical beams spaced 2 to 4 feet apart. There will be a heavy horizontal beam across the vertical ones, and other heavy beams that rest on the beam on the walls, and they run the width or length of the house. Any wall material then is "hung" from this heavy structure, and removing the wall material, or cutting openings in it, will not affect the structural strength of the building. You must not, of course, cut any of the vertical beams.

With post-and-beam construction you can install large windows, bay windows, doors, fireplaces and even "hanging closets" without being concerned about causing any weakening of the structure.

Ordinary houses will have 2 x 4 studs in the wall, usually spaced 16 inches on center. Some very recent structures are using what is called "Mod 24," and the 2 x 4s are spaced 24 inches on center. Homes that are quite old, say 50 or 60 years old, may have the studs 24 inches on center, but in those days the 2 x 4s used were a full 2 x 4 inches, while those today are finished to 1½ x 3½ inches. (Just a few years ago 2 x 4s were sized at 1⅝ x 3⅝ inches, and this can cause you problems. If you add to an existing wall, and use the new, smaller 2 x 4s in a wall with the larger ones, you will have to add shim strips of ⅛ or ¼ inch hardboard to one face to make them flush with the 2 x 4 studs already in the wall.)

To determine if a wall is or is not load-bearing, go up in the attic, if you have one, and see which way the ceiling joists run. Any wall (interior) that runs at right angles to the joists will be a load-bearing wall, holding up the joists. If a wall runs parallel to the ceiling joists, it will not be load-bearing.

Why is it important for you to know whether or not a wall is load-bearing? When you make an opening, as for a pass-through bar, in a non-load-bearing wall, you simply frame it with single 2 x 4s. If it is a load-bearing wall, however, you must open the wall to run a double 2 x 4 down to the sill plate on the floor on each side of the opening. The double studs support a "header," which is a double 2 x 4, 2 x 6 or 2 x 8 placed *on edge* across the top

With your planning done, as described in Chapter 1, the next step is to determine where it might be necessary to cut through a wall, and to figure whether the wall is load-bearing or non-load-bearing. Note that walls have been stripped inside.

This is "post-and-beam" house under construction. Generally the heavy ceiling beams will be exposed, and the underside of the roof decking is the ceiling surface. Wall beams also may be exposed, or walls will be noticeably thicker at windows and doors.

Older homes may have wall studs spaced 24 inches on center, rather than more recent 16 inches. A return to the 24-inch spacing is called "Mod-24", and is being employed to save on lumber. (Photo courtesy Western Wood Products Association)

Opening in non-load-bearing wall is simply framed in, but wall that is load-bearing requires double studs at sides of opening down to base plate, and header across top made of doubled 2-inch lumber.

Framing for Non-Load-Bearing Wall

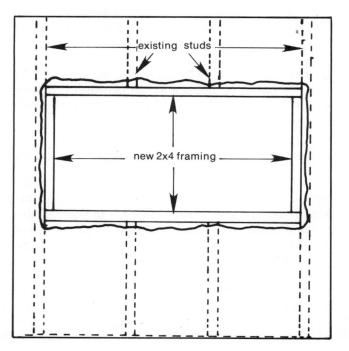

existing studs

new 2x4 framing

Framing for Load-Bearing Wall

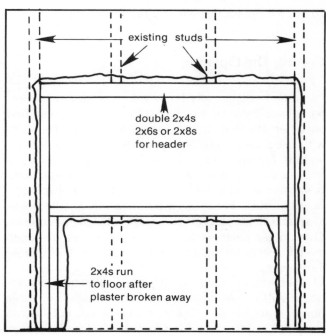

existing studs

double 2x4s
2x6s or 2x8s
for header

2x4s run
to floor after
plaster broken away

of the opening. Because the double thickness of 2-inch stock is not as wide as the studs, the headers must be spaced apart with strips of hardboard or plywood, or even old lath if you have some. The idea is to make the faces of the header flush with the edges of the 2 x 4s in the wall.

If you don't have an attic, or if the room is on the first floor and you can't determine which way the floor joists run in order to judge if the wall is load-bearing, it's a pretty safe bet that any wall that runs the long way of the house will be a load-bearing partition. The floor and ceiling joists almost always run the narrow way of a structure. This means that any wall that runs down the center, or near the center, of the house will be one that supports the ceiling joists—and thus is load-bearing.

Even with a load-bearing wall, it seldom is necessary to support the ceiling while you cut an opening and frame it. The exceptions, where a shore (shoring support) would be needed, would include openings 10 or more feet long, or an opening in an exterior wall. When such support is necessary, and we recommend against it unless you have had some experience in structural remodeling, you need to add a length of 2 x 10 or 2 x 12 on the floor, and another against the ceiling. Then cut shores (4 x 4s cut just a bit longer than the height from the 2-inch plank on the floor to the one on the ceiling). Alternately, cut the 4 x 4s about ¼ inch shorter than the distance and use wooden shingles as wedges under the 4 x 4s, driving two under each one, facing each other so they jam the 4 x 4 tightly against the ceiling. Don't overdo this or you could damage the ceiling. The idea is to provide a means of distributing the weight over a fairly large area of the floor and ceiling. It's rather obvious you'll need help to hold the 2 x 10 or 2 x 12 plank up there against the ceiling.

Cutting The Opening

When you actually break into a plaster or plasterboard wall there are two things to remember. First, find out where the studs are by tapping on the wall. The studs will have a solid sound, the spaces in between will sound hollow. Tapping on the wall is the most reliable way to find studs. So called "Stud finders" are magnetic compasses that are supposed to point at nails that hold plasterboard to studs. However, if the magnetic needle points to a metal electric box instead, you could have a problem. Cut from the center of the opening you wish to make, to the left and to the right toward the studs that will frame the opening.

Second, no matter what you do, plaster or plasterboard will create dust that will go through the whole house. You can't eliminate the dust problem, but you can minimize it. If there are doors that can be closed to seal off

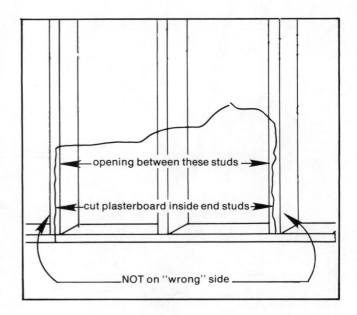

opening between these studs

cut plasterboard inside end studs

NOT on "wrong" side

the room, close them; then run masking tape all around the joint between the door and frame, including between the door and floor. Also mask off all cold and hot-air registers—don't just close them. Otherwise dust will be pulled into the cold-air returns and circulated to every room in the house. This occurs with forced-air heat, of course; if you have steam or hot-water heat, the problem doesn't exist.

If you are remodeling your living room in warm weather, open a window and set a fan in it blowing out. Try to have a second window open in the room to provide fresh air that circulates through the room. Even with the precautions described, there will be times when a respirator will be a necessity as the room fills with dust. It's amazing how much dust and dirt gets inside walls—waiting for you to release it, along with the plaster dust that you are bound to create.

Pass-Throughs

When you make a pass-through for a counter or bar, there is no "standard" height. Table tops are 30 inches high, but if you use stools, as at a bar or counter, that height would be much too low. A "stand-up" bar will be 39 or 40 inches from the floor, and this generally is the height of a bar where stools are used. If you are taller than average, you might be tempted to make any counter higher to suit you. The opposite would be true if you are short. This would be fine if you intended to live in the same house all your life, but most people live in a home only a few years, then move to another. If you make counters or bars too high or too low, you will be able to sell the house only to people in your height range, and that could restrict your selling market. Try to keep the counters and bars about 39 inches, and anything that is to be table height to about 30 inches.

When you cut the studs in a wall to make an opening, after removing the plasterboard or lath and plaster, be sure to cut them shorter by the thickness of the single or double 2 x 4 you will install. The same is true at the top of the opening; cut the studs shorter by a single or double thickness (or the width of the 2 inch stock that will be used for the header at the top of the opening).

If you are careful when removing plasterboard, you can salvage some pieces to fill in across the header spaces. The easiest way to do this is to cut down parallel to the wall studs. The joints can be taped or, with paneling, simply nailed to the joists to provide a surface flush with the rest of the wall.

Using a Flush Door

One quick and easy way to build a pass-through counter in a non-load-bearing wall is to use a flush door. These doors are thin plywood "skins" over a framework, and are relatively lightweight. You can buy these doors as "seconds," which means there is a flaw in the grain or color of the plywood so it cannot be sold as a door. Standard height (length) for a door is 6 foot 8 inches, and widths range from 24 inches for closet doors, to 30 or 32 inches for interior doors, and 36 inches for exterior doors. These doors can be shortened an inch or two at top and bottom, and about 1 inch on each edge. If you get the width you want, you need only cut the length. If you want to cut more than a couple of inches you'll cut into the hollow core of the door. Then, if you have some woodworking experience, you can cut the block from the cut-off piece and fit it into the open end of the door, holding it

Quick way to make a counter in a wall opening is with flush doors. Counter can be used for snacking, then converts to handy bar. (Photo courtesy Wall Covering Information Bureau)

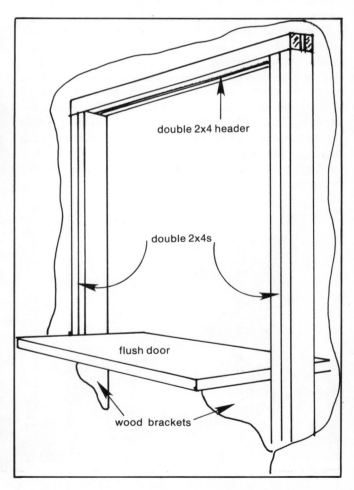

Plasterboard or other wall covering is removed, then opening for pass-through is framed. Flush door rests on horizontal 2 x 4, is supported by wood (or metal) brackets on either side of wall. Place brackets so they can be screwed to studs.

23

When you cover a counter for pass-through—or a bar top— use modern nonflammable contact adhesive and eliminate worry of fire hazard, and very objectionable odor. Some fumes from older flammable adhesives can be noxious. (Photo courtesy Borden Chemical Co.)

with glue. The simplest construction, of course, is to plan the pass-through counter to utilize the full size of the door.

Cover the edges and surface of the door with plastic laminate (Formica, Micarta, Textolite, etc.), applying it with contact adhesive. You can purchase contact adhesive with a water base, so there is no fire hazard as there is with the older types of adhesives with volatile, highly flammable solvents. To laminate, you apply strips to the door edge first, then trim or file it flush with the top. The top piece of the laminate goes on last, and covers the joint between the laminate and the edge of the counter. This minimizes problems caused by liquid getting into the joint.

There is no tougher or longer-wearing surface than ceramic tile, and with modern mastic adhesives and grouts, any do-it-yourselfer can create a beautiful counter. There is practically no limit to styles and colors available in ceramic tile. (Photo courtesy Tile Council of America)

As an alternative, cover the counter top and edge with ceramic tile. This material comes in an almost endless variety of colors, patterns and sizes, and is applied with mastic. When the mastic has set, usually overnight so the volatile solvents have evaporated, grout is wiped on to fill the joints between the tiles. Be sure the grout is the type use for floors or countertops, rather than the softer material used for walls. Somewhat more expensive than standard grout is the epoxy type that not only is very tough, but is stain-resistant. It comes in colors for unusual effects; for example, a yellow grout in brown tile.

Closing In

If the project you have in mind as the first step in the room remodeling is the closing of an unused door, start by carefully prying off the trim on both wall faces, then the inside casing. You want to be careful not just to try to salvage the trim and casing—which is a good idea—but to minimize any damage to the wall.

You now will have an opening framed by 2 x 4 studs, with a header of doubled 2 x 4s at the top. Cut a length of 2 x 4 to fit across the bottom of the opening, and one at the top. Measure both distances, because they may not be the same.

Now measure the distance between the header and the floor and deduct the thickness of two 2 x 4s (top and bottom plate). Cut three studs this length and assemble them to the top and bottom plate, using 16 penny box nails. In modern carpentry box nails are used almost ex-

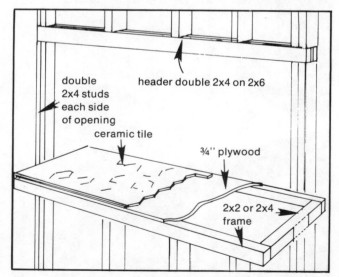

double 2x4 studs each side of opening

ceramic tile

header double 2x4 on 2x6

¾'' plywood

2x2 or 2x4 frame

Tile-covered counter shown is in load-bearing wall, so header of double 2 x 4s (or larger) is installed across top of opening. Note that header ends rest on double studs. Because of weight of ceramic tile, counter is assembled from lumber and ¾-inch plywood.

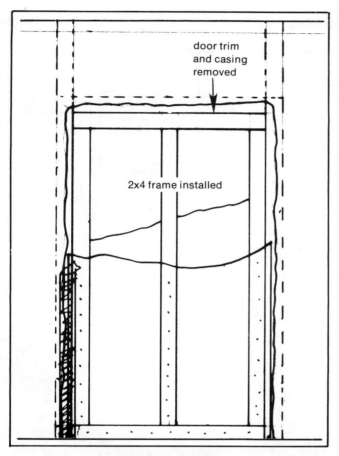

Unused door is closed in by first removing trim and casing, then assembling "frame" of 2 x 4s that is spiked inside opening. Plasterboard then is nailed over opening, joints in plasterboard are taped and smoothed with compound.

the straightedge, then snap it along the score. Don't saw plasterboard; this is one of the big dust-creating operations that some novice carpenters get into. It can cause a lot of "misunderstandings" with others in the family who have to clean the dust that seems to be on and in everything.

After the plasterboard has been nailed in place, wipe taping compound down the joints, press on joint tape, smoothing it firmly with a joint knife that you can buy where the tape and joint compound are sold. Don't add anymore joint compound; the joint should look as though it does not have enough tape. An amateur generally makes the mistake of applying too much compound, which must be sanded to smooth and level it. And this really makes clouds of dust. If you do apply too much joint compound, don't sand it. Instead, use a damp cellulose sponge and wipe down the rough spots. Keep rinsing the sponge in a bucket of water to flush out the joint compound.

If you are going to paint over the joints, apply compound two more times, feathering the final application about 8 or 10 inches across the joint. But if you are going to apply paneling to the wall, the one application with the compound is sufficient. All you want to do is seal the joint against dust.

An alternate method of closing off an unused interior door, and quite a bit simpler, is to make it a "book case." Buy some of the attractive wall-mounted metal standards that are available in lengths from 2 to 6 feet, in 2-foot increments. Screw the standards to the door frame, fit the metal brackets in the slots in the standards (they are spaced 1 inch apart so shelves can be arranged to suit) then slide on shelves you can buy, or cut your shelf from 1-inch shelving lumber or ¾-inch plywood.

The advantage of the book shelf closing is that the shelves can be removed when you sell the house, or if you

clusively in place of the regular nails that once were "standard." Box nails are thinner than regular nails, so drive more easily and have less tendency to split the wood. Drive two nails through the top and bottom plate into the three studs. Lift this assembly into the door opening and spike it (with 16 penny box nails) to the floor, the header and the two side studs.

The next step is to cut a piece of plasterboard to fit the opening on each side, then nail them with plasterboard nails. Dimple each nail by hitting it just hard enough to recess it below the surface, but not hard enough to break the paper on the plasterboard. Before applying the plasterboard, check to see if it will be necessary to nail on a shim on one or both sides of the frame you made in order to make the plasterboard flush with the existing plasterboard or lath and plaster. For interior walls we suggest ⅜-inch plasterboard, which is heavy enough to do the job, yet is relatively light and so can be easily handled. Plasterboard is cut with the aid of a straightedge and a linoleum or other heavy-duty knife. Score it the length of

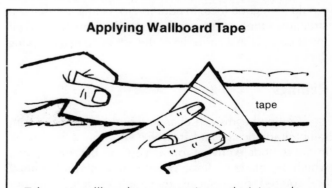

Applying Wallboard Tape

Take your wallboard tape, center it over the joint and press the tape firmly, into the bedding compound with your wallboard knife held at a 45° angle. The pressure should squeeze some compound from under the tape, but enough should be left for a good bond.

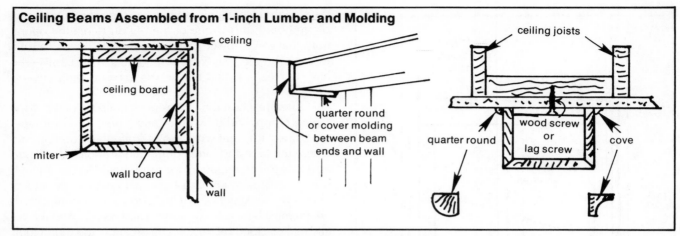

Ceiling Beams Assembled from 1-inch Lumber and Molding

You can make your own beams from 1-inch lumber. Beams are simply boxes with two sides and bottom that are nailed to length of lumber that is spiked to ceiling joists. Joint between "beams" and ceiling and wall is trimmed with quarter-round or cove molding.

ever want to open the door again. And it surely provides needed book shelf space when you are looking for every bit of storage space.

A third way to eliminate the door is to remove the door and close in the wall on the opposite side of the wall, and "build in" a book case in the opening. Like the room divider described later in this chapter, the book case can have an arched or "vaulted" top, or can be left square. Fit plasterboard or plywood inside the opening to cover studs on each side of the opening. It then will be necessary to use tape and compound on the outside corners created so the book case will appear as a neat recess in the wall. The wall back can be ⅜-inch plywood to match the thickness of the plasterboard in the wall. If you don't have members in the family who tend to hurl books onto shelves, you can use plasterboard for the back. It should be fastened to the shelves with plasterboard nails; which means the shelves will be fixed in place, rather than being adjustable. It would be a good idea, in addition to nailing, to use construction adhesive at the shelves. Apply a narrow bead on the shelves with a cartridge of the adhesive in a caulking gun.

Ceilings

Ceiling beams can change the character of a room rather dramatically, and are fine if you want a rustic look in the remodeled living room. You can buy the beams, which are made of dense polyurethane plastic, grained and colored so realistically that you can't tell them from the real thing without a close look.

You also can make the beams yourself, nailing 1-inch lumber to a 2 x 4 that is spiked to the ceiling joists. If the ceiling is in poor shape and you are going to have to cover it anyway, the beams are ideal. You then can nail

Ceiling beams change character of room quite dramatically and are ideal if you want a living room with a rustic atmosphere. Lightweight simulated beams of polyurethane are sold in most lumberyards and home centers, and are easy to install.

up strips of fresh plasterboard between the beams, or attach furring strips to which ceiling tile is stapled and glued. Ceiling tile comes in a variety of patterns, and some even has the appearance of rough plaster, which goes very well with rustic beams.

Storage Walls

If the room is large enough so that you can shorten it a couple of feet, a framework covered with paneling might be the answer to generous but hidden storage. This is especially true if you install a fireplace (see the chapter on fireplaces); the fireplace can be recessed and the wall brought out flush with the face of the fireplace, or even beyond.

The framework of the wall can be 2 x 4s or 2 x 2s; for both strength and minimum space loss, set the 2 x 4s

Wall built around fireplace can be versatile area that will provide storage, secret compartments, drawers, cabinets, even a bar. Wall is framed from 2 x 4s, covered with wall paneling. (Photo courtesy Masonite Corporation)

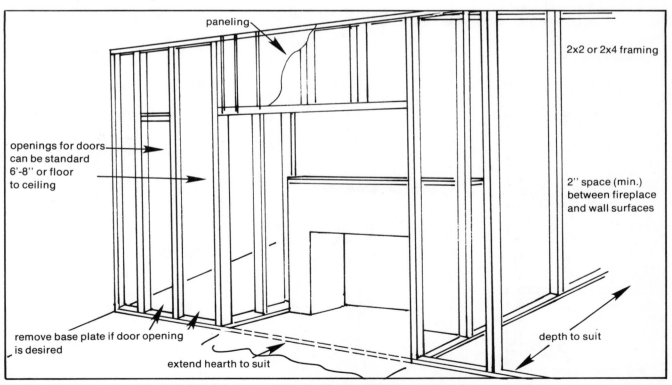

paneling

2x2 or 2x4 framing

openings for doors can be standard 6'-8'' or floor to ceiling

2'' space (min.) between fireplace and wall surfaces

remove base plate if door opening is desired

extend hearth to suit

depth to suit

Studs in framing around fireplace can be on 16 or 24-inch centers, and 2 x 4s can be positioned sideways to make wall only 1½ inches thick. For greater strength or to support shelves, position 2 x 4s in standard manner.

Storage Details

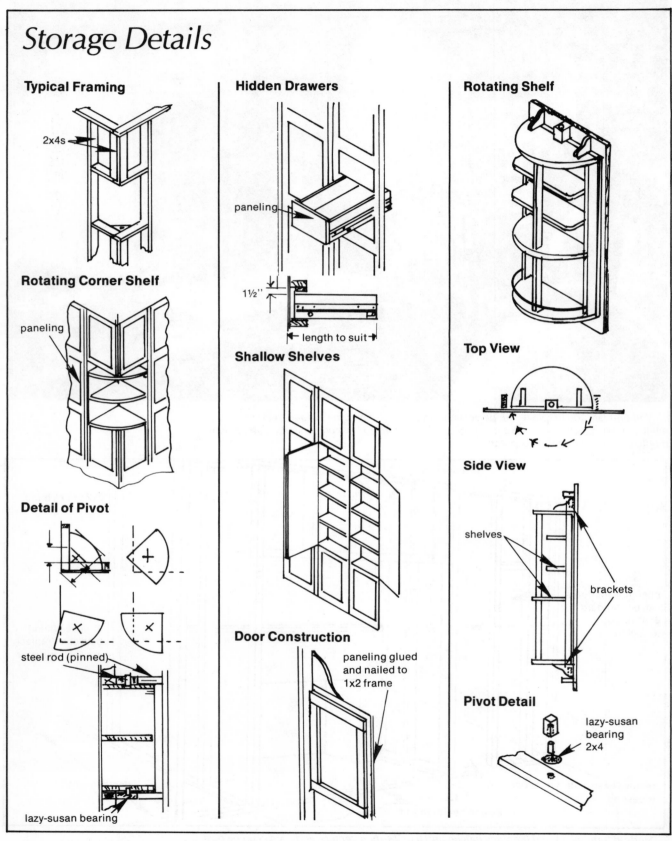

Typical Framing

2x4s

Rotating Corner Shelf

paneling

Detail of Pivot

steel rod (pinned)

lazy-susan bearing

Hidden Drawers

paneling

1½"

length to suit

Shallow Shelves

Door Construction

paneling glued
and nailed to
1x2 frame

Rotating Shelf

Top View

Side View

shelves

brackets

Pivot Detail

lazy-susan
bearing
2x4

Some suggestions for cabinets and other storage to be built into wall around fireplace. Adapt ideas to size and shape that suits you.

parallel to the wall surface rather than at right angles as is "standard." A variety of cabinets can be built into the wall, with the doors being fabricated of 1 x 2s to which the wall paneling is glued and nailed. The pin edge of the hinges will show, but there need be no exposed pulls or knobs if "Tutch-Latches" are used. These devices are pushed to close, then pushed again to open.

Drawers are no problem, being supported either on a piece of plywood as a shelf, or by ball-bearing extension slides that screw to the drawer sides and to the inside of the supporting frame.

If there is an outside corner in the wall assembly, say next to the fireplace, a "swing-out" shelf can be made by using "lazy-susan" hardware that is sold in most hardware stores, or by mail order from companies that sell supplies to do-it-yourself craftsmen. A swing-out shelf also can be built in the flat portion of the wall. Either of these "secret" compartments would make a fine bar, and would be out of sight when not in use. For a final touch, if you have some experience in hanging doors, use "invisible" hinges, such as those made by the Soss Company. You then would have no hinges or pulls exposed.

Note also that the wall would permit wiring special lights, and a dimmer switch would make the fireplace a real "mood" area. The fireplace, by the way, could be a real one, or you could build a realistic one that had an electric log in it.

While the area shown is only a couple of feet deep, where the floor space is available you could make the space behind the paneled walls deep enough for a small darkroom for the photo enthusiast, or a full-size bar could be hidden behind the wall, and exposed only by opening sections of the paneling with doors made from the paneling. A wall like this can be any of a hundred things, and only your imagination and wood working skills limit your choice.

Adding Space

How about a major structural change to add space to the room? A bay window might be your solution. To add floor space, get a bay that starts at the floor and goes up. If you just want a visual impression of increased space, install a bay that is 18 inches or 2 feet off the floor. It will make an extra seat as well as completely changing the character of the room.

An alternate to the bay is a "hanging closet." You probably have seen this kind of construction several times, but never gave a thought to how it was created. The closet is built by projecting the floor joists out a couple of feet to provide a floor on which a small extension of the

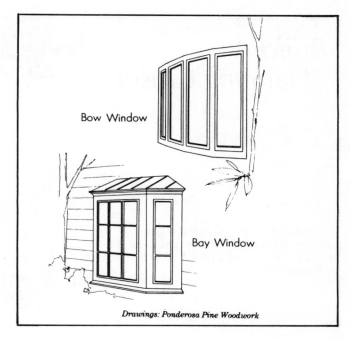

Bow Window

Bay Window

Drawings: Ponderosa Pine Woodwork

Prefinished wood windows are factory-assembled in complete easy-installing units, with all hardware mounted and ready for immediate operation. Shown here are the casement units formed into a bow combination installation.

Build A "Hanging Closet"

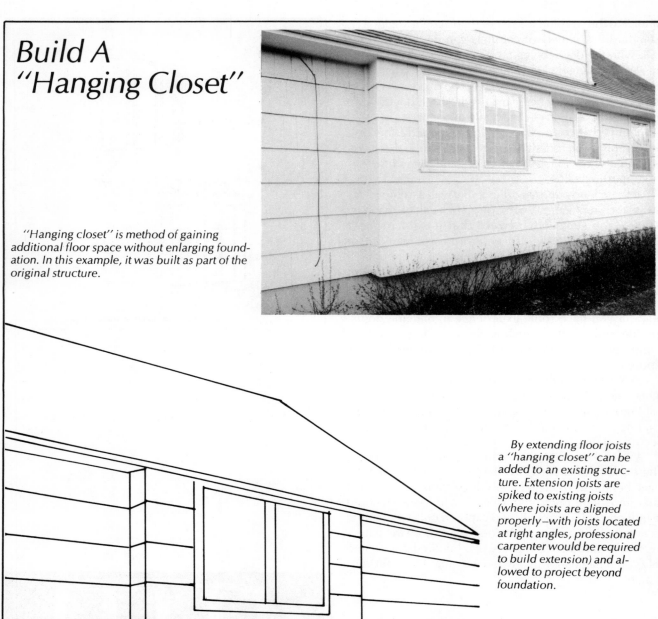

"Hanging closet" is method of gaining additional floor space without enlarging foundation. In this example, it was built as part of the original structure.

By extending floor joists a "hanging closet" can be added to an existing structure. Extension joists are spiked to existing joists (where joists are aligned properly—with joists located at right angles, professional carpenter would be required to build extension) and allowed to project beyond foundation.

at least
6 foot overlap

floor joists for
"hanging closet"
spiked to
existing joists

no more than
3 feet projects
beyond foundation

Before: If you have hanging closet in your home, it may have boxed-in soffit above. If header extends across closet to frame in windows, sliding glass door could easily be installed with minor structural changes.

After: Sliding glass door "opens" room and provides more light and even a view, makes area seem larger than it is.

room is built. While this usually is done when a home is built, you can add the joist extensions by opening the outside wall and then bolting the beam extensions to the existing joists. Don't overdo this: about 3 feet is the practical limit, with about 5 or 6 feet of the new joists extending back along the existing joists, and bolted to them.

If your house has an overhang on the edge of the roof, you are in luck, as no roof needs to be built for the hanging closet. Which might be one way of determining how far out you want to extend the floor. If you don't have a roof overhang, you'll have to build a small roof and cover it with the same kind of roofing material as on the main roof.

A hanging closet also is a good location for a sliding glass door, and if the extended closet already exists in your house, consider the light and ventilation such a door will provide. In the example shown there was a hanging closet that had had two windows put in. The sliding glass door was selected to be just less than the width of the windows. This assured that the existing header over the windows could be utilized as a header for the door. The same situation would be ideal also for a bay window. With an existing header, the bay could be fitted in place and studs fitted on either side to fill in, along with insulation. The outside then is finished off with sheathing and siding to match the rest of the house.

If any of these projects are a little beyond your skills, then have a contractor or carpenter make the rough opening and install the sliding glass door or the bay window.

You then could finish by installing the insulation, sheathing and siding, and trim on the inside. If a bay requires a 3-surface roof, you better let a carpenter build it unless you have had some experience in roof layout and construction.

Back inside the room you certainly can make built-ins. These basically are boxes built of ¾-inch plywood. They can have lift-up lids, or swing-open doors like cabinets, and are covered with the paneling used on the walls. Make seats 18 inches high; 16 inches if you use 2-inch cushions. Cabinets above the seat can be just about any size or shape you want them. Storage for a stereo set could be the function of such a cabinet, and the speakers could be fitted inside the bench and spaced to give the maximum stereo (or quadraphonic) sound.

Does someone in the family have a "green thumb" and love to grow plants? One end of the living room could be made into an "indoor greenhouse" by building a wall with arched (or square to simplify the job) openings. The indoor garden would add to the decor of the room or, on some occasions the area could be closed off with bamboo drops or even cloth drapes. Construction of the wall for the greenhouse is less complicated than the "fireplace wall," and could be an accent wall of paneling. It would not be necessary to have the whole room paneled.

If you'd like to make a niche for a couch or love seat, build another kind of wall, again with either straight or arched tops. The wall for the niche is made of 1x4s over which sheets of tempered hardboard are glued and

Change Your Space...

Built-in seating consists of carpet-covered plywood frame covered with carpet. Carpet then extends up the wall to emphasize unified effect. (Allied Chemical Corp.)

Niche for couch or love seat is created by building lightweight wall of 1 x 4s with hardboard on both sides. Recess built into framing has patterned hardboard to give color and accent to set off that part of room. (Photo courtesy Marlite Div. Masonite)

Plywood boxes covered with wall paneling make attractive seats, provide additional storage. Ready-made cushions with easy-clean plastic covers are sold in specialty and department stores, as well as large mail-order outlets.

One end of the living room could be set off by simple wall of framing and paneling. Floor in area should be easy-clean vinyl or ceramic tile, if plants are to be cultivated.

Create A New Wall

Paneled wall for "indoor greenhouse" can be assembled on frame of 2 x 4s (2 x 3s to save space), with arched openings. For simpler construction, make tops of openings square, but have them higher than standard (6 feet 8 inches) height of door opening. (Photo courtesy U.S. Plywood)

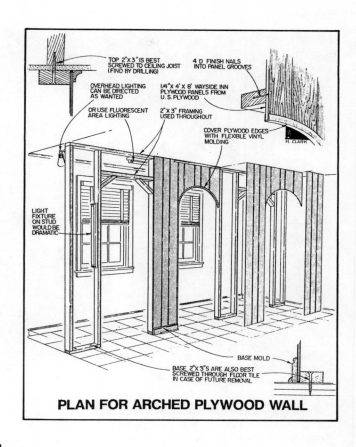

PLAN FOR ARCHED PLYWOOD WALL

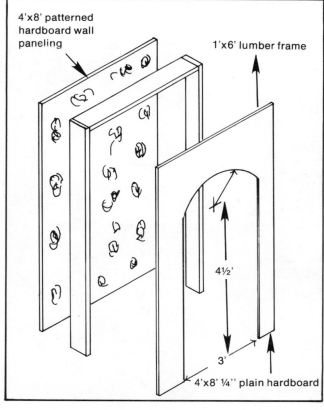

U-shape box has no frame on floor, must be supported by another box at right angles, or if single, must be held to ceiling or wall. Frame at bottom would permit nailing box to the floor.

Before

If you are ready to add a room addition, make it a "complete" living room like this 17 x 19-foot area added to create L-shape with existing kitchen-dining room. Room contains fireplace, entertainment center and bar. Book shelves and tables provide handy place for books and magazines for those members of the family who enjoy reading. (Photos courtesy Azrock Floor Products)

After

Open box built into outside wall provides storage for firewood, eliminates need to go outdoors in bad weather. (Photo courtesy Forest Fiber Products—Forestex 2-tone Roughsawn Siding)

Firewood Cabinet

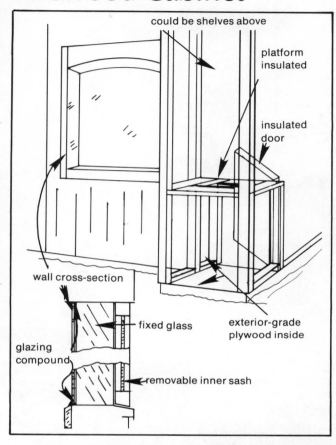

Firewood storage is projection of building at ground level, and basically is heavily insulated box with insulated door. Space above box could be cabinet or shelves. Window installation is fixed pane outside, removable pane inside, which provides storm sash and easy cleaning.

nailed. The inside areas of the arches are paneled with some of the new "decorator" panels that come in brilliant colors and exciting patterns.

Wiring could be concealed inside the hollow posts of the wall, and special lighting installed. The tops of the arches (or square openings) could be closed off with translucent plastic, and lights installed above the panels. The plastic is available in a wide range of colors, and a dimmer switch to control the light intensity would offer a dramatic setting.

A wood-burning fireplace is a very practical thing, just great to take the chill off a room in fall or spring when you don't want to run the furnace. But bringing in the firewood can be a chore. Especially if it's raining or snowing. The solution is to have log storage built into an outside wall, with access by a well-insulated door. The logs stay fairly dry in the semi-enclosed storage, and you don't have to go outside to get them.

This requires cutting a hole in the wall, and the inside of the compartment can be built to look like a cabinet or a built-in seat, depending on the size and shape of the storage. Just be sure that all surfaces exposed to the outside are well insulated.

An added feature to this storage would be a window adjacent to it. The outside glass is set in a frame and puttied (by using modern glazing compound), while the inside sash actually is a storm sash. This minimizes heat loss, and the inner sash is readily removed to be cleaned. The inner surface of the outside glass also could be cleaned, and there would be only one surface that would require that you go outside to clean.

When you are planning a project, keep in mind that you not only want it as simple to build as possible, but easy to keep clean. Which means, in the case of the outside glass just described, it should be easily removed and replaced in case of breakage.

Lightweight paneling strips of cedar create several unusual effects: herringbone pattern on one wall, sunburst pattern on another. Flexible strips are just 1/9 inch, can even be bent to fit curved wall next to ceiling. (Photo courtesy Pope and Talbot)

3. Accent Walls

You can change the size and shape of a room with color. Which means an inexpensive, easily applied coat of paint can work wonders. But don't just paint the room one color; one wall can be lighter than the others so it will seem closer. Or paint a wall dark to have it look farther away. Try using one of the design rollers to apply a pattern to the wall and it will "smile" at you in any of a dozen patterns. Because the pattern is applied with paint, it can be covered with another coat of paint when it comes time to change the decor of the room—even easier than removing "strippable" wallpaper.

Paneling and Molding

Painted walls in combination with one paneled wall create a striking effect. It is not even necessary to panel a complete wall. One section of a wall, maybe that part set off by a large window, can be paneled for a special corner in the living room.

Special Effects

As shown in one photo, the paneled wall can be complemented by ceiling beams (as described in Chapter 2) that have been stained the same color as the paneling. Another bit of decorating magic is the use of molding to cover the joints between sheets of plasterboard, rather than taping them and applying compound. There are many shapes and sizes of molding; they can be run on the vertical joints of plasterboard, and in the corner between wall and ceiling. You can apply the strips of molding even if the wall has already been taped and is smooth. Just space them equidistant across the wall about 3 or 4 feet apart. The vertical lines will make the wall appear higher.

Conversely, if you run the molding strips horizontally, the wall will look wider. If the molding is run horizontally, then the paneling also should be run with the lines parallel to the floor; it too will lengthen the wall visually. The same molding that is used on the painted wall can be used to trim the paneling, but it should

Design rollers let you apply a variety of patterns to a wall to make it the focal point of a living room. Since it is paint, another coat of paint over it "removes" it so you can apply another color or pattern. (Photo courtesy Rollerwall, Inc.)

Striking effect is created by combining painted walls with one that is paneled. Here just one section of a wall is paneled; the rest is painted. Ceiling beams complement paneling.

First step in applying figured paneling that has appearance of wallpaper, but easy maintenance of paneling, is to apply adhesive to back of each panel.

Panel is then fitted in place in corner of room, pressed to wall to bond it securely.

be stained to match the paneling. A room with walls that are both paneled and painted will have just a touch of informality.

If you want a more dramatic look with your paneling, apply it diagonally across the wall. This kind of application does take more time, and you waste a lot of material, so if you have economy in mind, better go vertical or horizontal with the sheets of paneling.

You can also use strips of solid wood for paneling. Applying these strips involves less wasted material and, since you are working with relatively narrow strips, any error you make can be corrected without too much loss of material. The solid-wood strips will not be long enough to go the full width of the wall; they will have to be pieced. This is another time-and-temper saver if you make a cut at the wrong angle. You can simply cut off the angled end square and fit it somewhere else in the pattern.

Still another application is to make a V-shape on the wall with paneling. Do you want the point of the Vee up or down? To accurately determine this, clear the wall that is to be paneled and lay out V-shape you want. Use paint stripes to draw the Vee, first with the point up, then with it down. Use two colors of paint so you can stand back and see the difference that having the point up or down will make. How about having the point of the Vee to the left or

right? No reason why not; but paint your lines in first to be very sure it is the look you want.

Do you like the look of wallpaper but hesitate to apply it yourself? Do you want an accent wall that is easy to clean? Then plastic-coated panels are the answer. These panels come in standard 4 x 8-foot size, are available in a variety of patterns, and can be applied with adhesive like other types of paneling. The melamine-coated panels can have the joints sealed with matching metal trim, and the plastic coating wipes clean with a damp cloth. The adhesive application requires that the wall be in good condition, flat, smooth and clean.

Selection and Use

When creating an accent wall, there is no doubt that the easiest way to do the job is with paneling. But there can be pitfalls here also. Don't buy paneling by looking at a color brochure or an ad in a magazine. Great pains are taken to get the printed color to be as close to the color of the paneling as possible, but there can never be an absolute match.

A small picture also does not show the grain or pattern clearly enough to show you how it will look on your

Matching molding can be applied to cover vertical edge of panels; molding is nailed to wall.

Next panel is slipped into molding, and adhesive on back bonds it to wall. Molding and panels are alternated length of wall. (Photos courtesy Marlite Paneling)

wall. Go to a lumberyard, home center, or larger hardware store that has the paneling you are considering, and carefully examine the full sheet and the color. On the same principle, if you have a certain color of paint in mind for the wall, and a definite shade of material for drapes or curtains, take along a scrap of the cloth and a paint sample. Paint a scrap of wood or plasterboard, let it dry overnight and use it for the paint sample. You can't go by printed colors for paint anymore than you can for paneling.

Quite probably the showroom where the paneling is on display will have fluorescent lighting. This is all right if you will have fluorescent lamps in the living room, but not if you will be using incandescent lighting. If possible, get hold of a small sample of the paneling, take it and your paint and drape material to an incandescent lamp and see how they match or contrast.

Go outside with your samples and see how they look in natural light. Remember that the living room will be lighted by the sun during the daylight hours.

What kind of wall paneling should you consider? There are three basic types. Solid lumber is usually strips of tongue-and-groove softwood, because hardwood is incredibly expensive. The softwood can be stained a wood tone, or a touch of color can be applied. Which

means you can pretty well control the color you want. An exterior stain would be a good bet; use one of the oil types, or latex, with a touch of color but which is transparent enough so the wood grain shows through.

The second type of paneling is plywood. This is less expensive, usually, than solid paneling (you can buy 4 x 8-foot sheets of exotic rosewood for over 100 dollars apiece) and less than hardboard paneling. Plywood paneling is available in softwood and hardwood; that is, the face veneer is a hardwood. In the last few years there has been developed a method of embossing and coloring inexpensive imported hardwood to look like other hardwoods so the paneling is extremely attractive with a rich look.

The third type of wall paneling is the hardboard type. You can buy hardboard paneling ⅛-inch thick with a vinyl coating that is printed to look like wood. The coating scratches easily, and there is no doubt when you look at this paneling that it is cheap hardboard material. Its only redeeming quality is that it's cheap. But if you want your living room to look good for several years, stay away from this kind of paneling. Hardboard paneling ¼-inch thick is also available; it is available with an embossed wood grain and a two-tone finish. It looks good, wears well, and the variety of colors and patterns is great

Mirror tiles installed on one wall will make living room seem to be twice its actual size. Tiles can be small or large (Photo courtesy Masonite Corp.)

Quality textured hardboard paneling is two-toned to look much like real wood; in this case it's "Barnside" by Marlite Paneling.

Hardboard paneling here has look of real brick combined with wood strips. Adjacent wall is paneling that complements brick. (Marlite Paneling)

Simulated-brick paneling, or stone as here, is so realistic you have to look closely to tell it is not the real thing. (Photo courtesy Z-Brick)

Embossed paneling has surface that looks something like leather, combines well with more traditional wood paneling for unusual accent wall. (Photo courtesy Marlite Paneling)

Alternating panels give adjacent walls the look of marble slabs with wooden columns between. (Photo courtesy Marlite Paneling)

Narrow 16-inch panels are a lot easier to handle than more standard 48-inch-wide panels, so they could be your answer for easier working. Additional furring strips are required for application. (Photo courtesy Marlite Paneling)

To make wall look longer, apply paneling horizontally rather than usual vertical alignment, or use paneling like this with strong horizontal lines. (Photo courtesy U.S. Gypsum Co.; Wal-Lite)

Doors in paneled wall can conceal storage; here canned goods, but it could be bottles for the bar or other items. Tutch-Latches allow doors to be pushed to open, pushed to close, do not project.

enough so that you should be able to find a combination to suit any decor you have in mind.

This better hardboard paneling also can be obtained with a brick or stone look that is so authentic you can hardly tell it is not the real thing. You might get suspicious if you saw a brick or stone wall 15 or more feet long on the second floor of a house, but that would be the only real clue that it wasn't the genuine article.

A "sub-type" of hardboard paneling has a melamine coating. This plastic is extremely water-resistant, and is used for bathtub enclosures and other high-humidity areas. It now comes in such a variety of colors and patterns that it can be used as wallcovering in a living room, as described previously.

A further "sub-type" of hardboard paneling makes no pretense at being wood. Rather, it comes embossed with patterns such as leaves or flowers. Generally the paneling is a brown color, but can be painted to suit your color scheme. One very attractive method of finishing is to "two-tone" the paneling. You first brush or spray on a dark (or light) base coat, then when it is dry apply a contrasting color. When the second coat has set for about 15 minutes, you wipe it off, leaving the color only in the recesses of the embossed pattern. This "two-tone" or "antique" finish can be repeated in other colors in the future, when you want to change your color scheme.

A dramatic accent wall can be created by using alternate panels of wood-grain hardboard paneling and the embossed type. The embossed panels, if left their natural dark color, give the visual impression of recesses in the wall, producing a depth that a single type of paneling would not.

A somewhat similar look can be made with alternate panels of wood-grain hardboard (or plywood) and hardboard paneling that has a "plaster" or "stucco" finish. This paneling comes not only in the fairly standard 4 x 8-foot sheets, but in strips that are 16 inches wide and 8 feet long. This permits you to make a "beamed wall" look by using one 16-inch strip of wood-grained paneling to separate a 32 or 48-inch section of the plaster-look paneling.

The 16-inch panels are a lot easier to handle than the standard 48 x 96-inch sheets, so if you are not up to wrestling the full-size panels, the smaller ones will let you do the job. If the wall is in poor shape, you will have to nail on furring strips 16 inches on center, with a horizontal strip across the top and bottom, and one about halfway between. If you plan on using a base molding on the wall, use a 1 x 4 or 1 x 6 for the bottom furring strip to provide ample nailing surface.

To make a short wall look longer, apply paneling horizontally, or use a paneling with strong horizontal lines. This kind of paneling also lends itself to creating wall storage between the studs. This is only on an inside wall, of course. Remove the plaster or plasterboard, then make "doors" of the paneling, using "Tutch-Latches" to eliminate the need for pulls. Nail ¾ x 1-inch cleats to the studs to support shelves of ½ or ⅜-inch plywood. Just set the shelves on the cleats; don't fasten them. This will allow removing one or more shelves to allow the storage of tall items, then replacing the shelves when you have only short items to store.

When paint doesn't quite do the job, make a wall really dramatic by hanging panels of wood in frames on the wall. These oversize framed panels can be plywood or hardboard, or even a figured or wallpapered surface. Make the frames 16 x 64 inches, and three or four will cover a wall 12 feet long. Space the frames equidistant from each other and from the floor and ceiling.

The pieces of plywood or hardwood paneling, or sheets of hardboard, are framed with molding mitered at the corners. There is a broad range of shapes and sizes of molding, so you can give the removable panels any kind

Before:. This wall is painted, and absolutely without character. You can change its appearance with "hang-on" panels. (Western Wood Products Association)

After: Striking change in character of room is created by panels of plywood inside frames of molding. (Western Wood Products Association)

Molding is mitered 45 degrees at corners, much like giant picture frame to hold the paneling. (Western Wood Products Association)

Miter A Molding

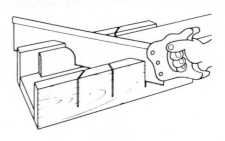

To cope a molding, make a 45 degree cut, angled so that a slanted raw edge shows from the front.

To miter a molding, start by cutting both ends on 45 degree angles in opposite directions.

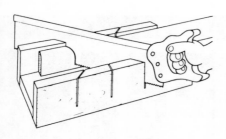

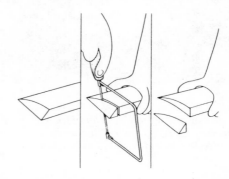

Cut straight back across the molding so that all of the slanted, raw wood is removed.

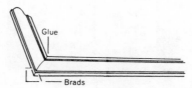

Glue

Brads

Glue the raw ends of both pieces together and secure the corner with brads.

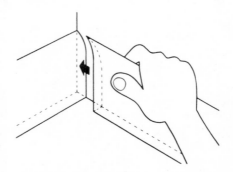

Remaining trimmed molding end will fit snugly to matching molding.

44

There is wide variety of moldings that can be used to frame hanging panels, from plain to ornate.

Framed panels are leveled, held by a couple of finishing nails at the top, just one at the bottom. This permits easy removal if you decide to change the wall, or to move the panels.

of character you want. Level the panels after you have them positioned, then attach them with just a few finishing nails through the molding and plaster into the wall studs. Recess the nails with a nail set and cover the heads with a bit of colored wood putty.

Installation Tip. When you strip an old wall of plaster or plaster board, with the intention of installing wall paneling, don't apply the paneling directly to the studs. Instead, first apply plasterboard. This does two important things: it provides fireproofing—the paneling may burn quickly, but the gypsum plasterboard will resist fire for a considerable period; it offers insulative benefits—foil-back wallboard adds reflective insulation, and the mass of the wallboard helps keep a room insulated from sounds that might easily pass through thin paneling.

Other Wall Coverings

For an accent wall that is both attractive and functional, apply simulated brick. This material is fireproof and you can cover a complete wall with it, or just make a fire wall behind a free-standing fireplace. The brick is applied with mastic, one unit at a time, then later can have a "grout" applied between each brick. The masonry is truly realistic, and can be applied by anyone who can use a level to start the first row, then space the other "courses" equally—but with just a bit of irregularity so the bricks look like a real brick wall with the natural minor errors that occur in a real bricklaying job.

If your living room is small and you'd like to make it look bigger, apply mirror tile to one wall. Small mirror tiles 12 inches square can be applied with panel adhesive from a caulking gun. Be sure the adhesive says it will adhere to glass.

An attractive accent wall can be made by applying simulated brick. The brick is fireproof, waterproof, looks so much like the real thing the wall will appear to be real masonry. (Photo courtesy Z-Brick Co.)

Simulated brick in stark white sets off fireplace, contrasting strongly with dark wall paneling. Brick provides fire wall to protect against heat from fireplace. (Photo courtesy Fireplace Institute)

Wall Treatments

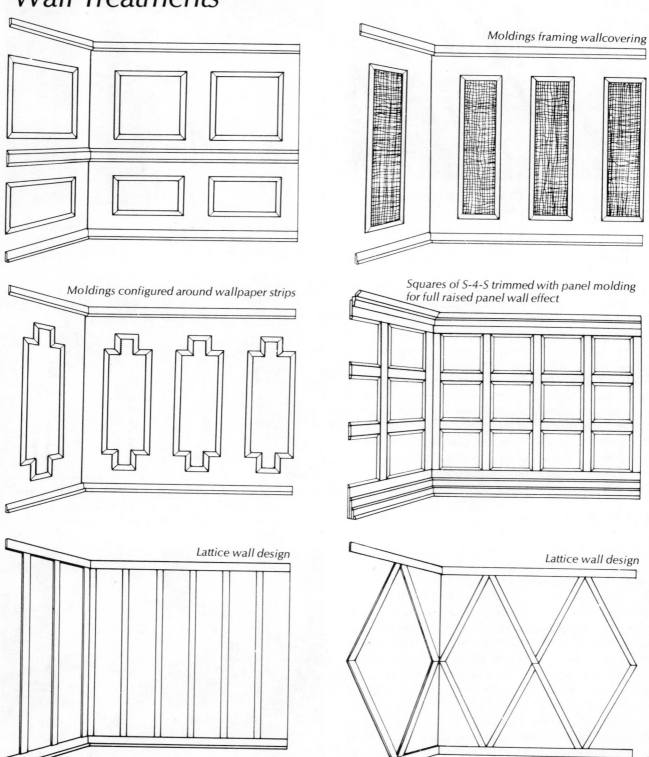

Moldings framing wallcovering

Moldings configured around wallpaper strips

Squares of S-4-S trimmed with panel molding for full raised panel wall effect

Lattice wall design

Lattice wall design

Ceiling trim (crown, bed or cove)

Chair rail (traditional height)

Base trim

Wainscot cap or plycap

Plywood, hardboard, or lumber paneling (high wainscot)

Applied molding for panel look

Traditional wall

Plate rail wall

Quarter Round S-4-S

Crown

Apply a texture to a wall that will hide cracks and damaged areas, completely change character of the wall. Texture paint can be applied with brush or trowel, variety of surfaces can be created. (Photos courtesy Z-Brick Co.)

If plain mirror might be too stark, check into the mirror tiles that have gold or silver veining. This kind of mirror still creates the visual doubling of the size of the room, but the touch of gold or silver mutes the reflection just a bit, and produces a glamorous feeling.

If you'd like a very special mirror wall, go to a glass shop and have them cut mirror tiles that are 2 feet square. This means that four tiles reach from floor to ceiling on a standard wall that is 8 feet high. But measure the height of the wall first; most so-called 8-foot ceilings will actually measure 7 foot 10 or 11 inches. This is because the room is framed to be 8 feet high, then the ceiling and floor are installed. If you go to the 2-foot mirror tiles, just have one row cut about ⅛ inch less than the height between 6 feet and the ceiling. The ⅛ inch allows for variations in the height of the wall, which is almost inevitable in an older home, and very possible in a new one. The gap between the upper edge of the top tile and the ceiling can be concealed with a wooden molding.

Be careful when nailing the molding. The safest bet is to nail into the ceiling joists, or at an angle to drive the nails up into the top plate of the wall. You are working around a lot of glass, so do this trim job when you are rested mentally and relaxed. Having your mind on something else while you are driving the nails into the molding could cause a slip of the hammer—and a considerable amount of broken glass.

How about something not quite paint and not quite paneling, but which changes the surface of a wall completely? Try a "texture" paint. This material is a thick paint, almost a thin plaster, that is painted on a wall, then textured with a trowel, a paintbrush or even a cellulose sponge. Depending on how you work the material the wall will have a stucco appearance, or troweled plaster or simply a "sandy" finish. The basic texture paint is white, but it can be tinted with colors to create some very spectacular effects.

When an old wall is stripped of covering and you intend to panel it, first apply wallboard as a fire and soundproofing barrier. Lightweight paneling will burn quickly, plasterboard, such as this foil-back type, is highly heat- and flame-resistant. (Photo courtesy U.S. Gypsum Co.)

Texture paint contrasts or blends with paneling, and can also be applied to ceiling to make it look completely new and different. Here it is troweled on wall for "Mediterranean" look.

4. Dramatic Lighting

For many years lighting was just functional; today, it's used for decorating a room as well—to set the mood of the room for your choice of activities. It's easy to decorate with lights, and often you can do it without changing any of the major wiring or fixtures in the room.

Dimmer Switch

The simplest way to "glamorize" your room lighting is to install a dimmer switch in place of the existing switch. Dimmer switches can be purchased at any hardware store. They can be used to replace almost any switch in your home. If the switch you're replacing happens to be a three-way switch (controls light in connection with another switch in another location), make sure you purchase a 3-way dimmer switch.

You can change the switch yourself; all you'll need is a small screwdriver. The first step is to remove the fuse or kick out the circuit breaker that powers that circuit. If you're not sure if the circuit is off, plug a lamp in the outlet before removing the fuse or turning off the breaker. Turn the light on, then go shut off the power—if the lamp goes out the circuit is off. If there are several people in the house it's a good idea to make up a small sign which says POWER OFF, WORKING ON ELECTRICITY. This can be taped over the fuse or circuit box to prevent anyone from turning the power back on before you're finished with the job.

When you're sure the circuit is shut off, remove the two screws that hold on the switch plate. Now take out the two screws that hold the switch in the box. Finally, unscrew the two screws that hold the wires to the switch. You may also have a ground wire run to the box containing the switch. If so, leave this connected. In some cases if the switch is a newer one, the wires will be fitted in holes

in the back of the switch. Release these wires by pressing a small screwdriver into the slots next to the wires. Instructions for doing this will be printed right on the switch. Now merely reverse the procedure to install the new three-way dimmer switch.

You only need one dimmer switch in a three-way circuit. The degree of brightness set by the dimmer switch remains the same; the other switch simply turns the current on and off at that setting.

First step is to pull the front control knob off of the switch. Then fasten the wires to the new switch. Place the switch back in the box and fasten it in place with the two screws at top and bottom. Make sure the switch is straight up and down and isn't sitting crooked in the box. Fasten the wall plate back in place. Incidentally, you may wish to purchase a wall plate of a different color to match the control knob of the switch. When the wall plate has been securely fastened in place, merely push the control knob back over the spindle. Now you're ready to turn the power back on.

Dimmer switch can be used to replace old existing switch. Makes room lighting much more versatile. First step is to remove fuse or flip circuit breaker and make sure power is off.

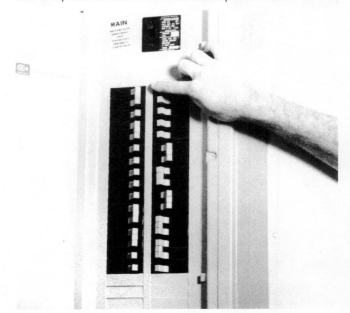

◄ *This stunning skylight requires preconstruction planning. The huge fireplace is surrounded by built-in seating and storage. Roof is heavily insulated with solid material on top of roof decking, while enormous skylight provides ample illumination whenever the sun shines. (Photo courtesy Tile Council of America)*

51

Fig. 4.1

1. Unscrew screws holding old switch box.

2. Remove old wires from switch.

3. Rewire in new switch.

4. Replace in box.

5. Add new cover plate.

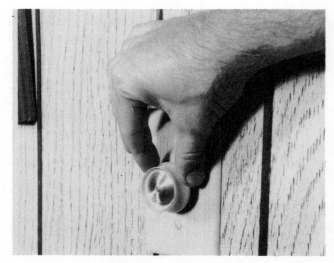

6. And press switch knob in place over spindle.

Installing a Chandelier

If you have old light fixtures in your living room or foyer, you might consider updating them with new more sophisticated fixtures, or fixtures that will complement your decorating scheme. In most cases the conversion is quite simple. Again shut off the power at the fuse or circuit-breaker box. Merely turning off the switch is not enough. Examine the top portion of the chandelier or fixture closely. The photos below illustrate the most common method of affixing these to the electrical box, and/or ceiling. Determine which method has been used and remove the old fixture or chandelier. Unscrew the screws holding the wires in place and remove these as well. Examine the wiring carefully while the fixture is removed to determine what condition the wiring is in. If it is old, cracked, etc., or the insulation is gone, you may wish to have an electrician in to determine how safe all your wiring is. In

1. The first step is to shut off power, then remove the old fixture.
2. Fasten new hanger strap to fixture box with screw provided. Then pull wires down through hole in middle of hanger strap.
3. Strip old wire back about ½ inch, and using twist-on connectors, fasten the wires together just as they were on old chandelier.

4. Push chandelier bell up over fixture box, and allow studs on hanger strap to protrude through holes in bell. Then turn on decorative nuts.

5. The finished unit.

minor cases re-wrapping the wire with tape is sufficient. Again, do not remove the grounding wire (normally green or bare copper) from the box if connected there. If there is a grounding wire connected to the old fixture, make sure you connect it to the green screw terminal or terminal marked ground on the new fixture. Then fasten the black wire to the brass screw terminal on the fixture and the white wire to the silver screw terminal. These must be in their proper places for the light to work properly. In many cases the fixture will have wires protruding from the socket base. To hook the fixture up merely fasten the black wire to black wire, and white wire to white wire; this should follow the same wiring scheme found in the old fixture. When you dismantle the fixture from the existing wires, note their locations and mark them with

a piece of tape if necessary so you can be sure you get the switching wires in the correct position. For most people the best method of fastening the wires together is to utilize "twist-on" connectors. In use the two wires are stripped back about ⅜th of an inch, then held together. Push the connectors down over the wire ends and twist clockwise until the connector is tight and secure on the wires. Then gently tug on each of the wires to make sure it is solidly anchored in place. Quick and easy, with none of the old fashioned taping, soldering, etc. But make sure there is no portion of a bare metal wire which could contact a metal portion of the fixture and cause a short.

With the wires connected, fasten the fixture in place using the holding devices packed with the fixture. Turn the electricity back on.

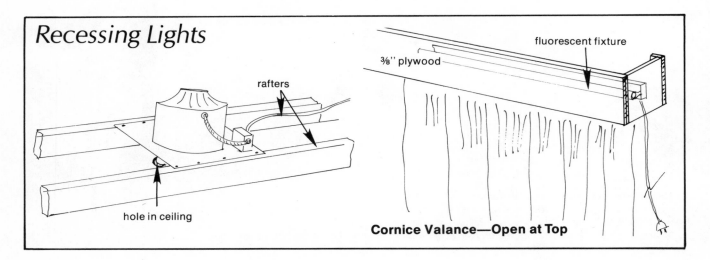

Recessed Lights

An even more impressive method of changing the lighting situation of your room is to add recessed lights. Recessed or hidden lights are fantastic for achieving special effects, and because they don't protrude down in the room they're out of the way and sort of blend into the decor. Because of this, many more of them can be utilized in a room than ordinary fixtures. There are many different kinds and styles, and they can be arranged around the room to light different portions of the room. They can be used as a sort of "light barrier" to determine the different activity areas of the room. For instance you can have lights which shine down directly over a chair for reading, or use dimmer switches as well to set up a party mood. You can also have recessed "spotlight" fixtures scattered around the room to light a special piece of furniture or wall hanging. To really brighten a room, use recessed fixtures shining against a light-colored drape across an en-

tire wall. There is almost no end to the effects that can be achieved in this manner.

Installing recessed fixtures is a job for the pro, both because of the electrical problems of determining how many fixtures can be added to a line as well as the mechanical problems of cutting the holes in the ceiling and installing the fixture properly.

Another way to achieve recessed lighting without all the hassle is to utilize it in combination with a drapery valance. If the valance is constructed with an open top, a fluorescent tube can often be placed in the valance and will throw a soft light up on the ceiling, lighting the room indirectly without any glare from a visible fixture. This can often be a simple carpentry job and utilize an outlet on the wall covered by the drapery.

One means of getting around all the problems of installing the recessed fixtures, but getting the same decorating results, is to utilize track lighting.

Dropped Ceilings For A New Look

1. Armstrong's Integrid ceiling begins with either metal or wood wall molding nailed at the desired height on all four walls. First, a chalk line is drawn around the perimeter of the room ¾-inches above the intended ceiling height to serve as a guide for molding. Panels are adjusted in length and width around the sides so that partial panels are equal on either end of the room, and full-sized panels are centered.

3. Once all main runners are in place, ceiling tiles are installed by starting in one corner. Tile is laid on the molding and a four foot cross-tee is snapped into the main runner. Then the tee is slid into a special concealed slot on the leading edge of the tile.

4. The rest of the ceiling is laid up similarly, with tiles and cross-tees inserted in the same way. All metal suspension hangers are completely concealed as the ceiling goes up.

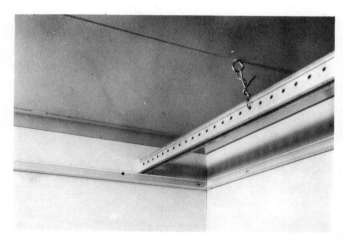

2. Integrid main runners are installed with hanger wires, with the first runner always located 26 inches out from the sidewall and the remaining units placed 48 inches on center, perpendicular to the direction of joists. The system is so simple that it takes no complicated measuring or room layout.

5. Finished ceiling looks solid.

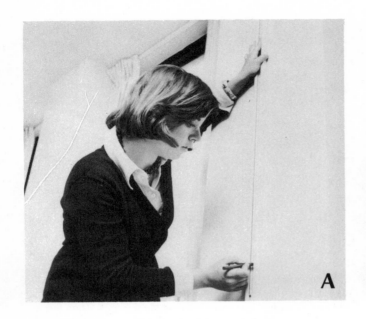

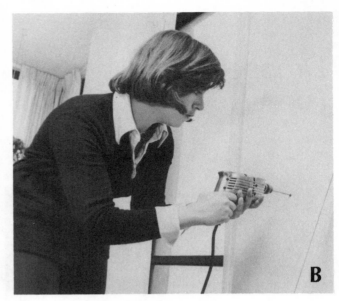

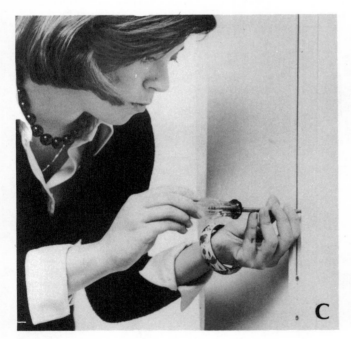

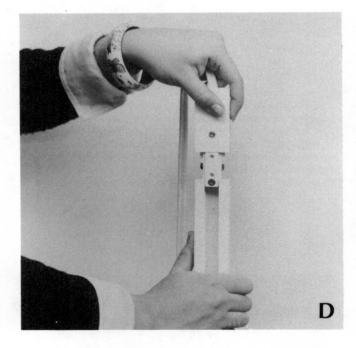

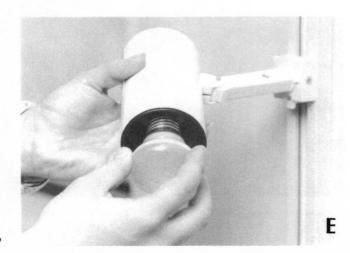

Install track lighting in five steps. (A) Place track on wall and mark fastening positions. (B) Drill holes. (C) Fasten track to wall with screws from kit. (D) Insert cord and plug connecter. (E) Once lamps are placed in the track, insert bulbs. (Halo Lighting).

Track Lighting

Track lighting will provide a constantly changing play of lights. The several lamps can be moved across the wall, or up and down. The reflectors can be adjusted to point up or down, or any angle between. They also can be positioned horizontally to suit. Installing track lighting is an easy job that requires only a few measurements, perhaps drilling a few holes and installing a few screws. (See step-by-step photos.)

The system consists of a fully grounded electrified track and individual lampholders. Adaptors permit attachment of the lampholders to the track at any point, automatically making the necessary electrical connections. The lampholders themselves are available in a variety of styles and can be moved along the track much as a clothespin can be moved on a clothes line.

Installation of the system is simple. First determine where you want light directed; it is recommended that the light strike the object illuminated at a 30 to 45 degree angle. Thus, for overhead lighting in a room with a 9 foot ceiling, the track should be approximately 3 to 3½ feet away from the wall. For an 8 foot ceiling, 2 to 2½ feet should be about right.

The mounting steps shown require only about a half-hour, assuming a wall or ceiling outlet is nearby. Modifications to existing wiring or addition of multiple tracks, of course, require additional time.

Today's lighting provides much more than just light to see by. It can be used to set the entire mood of a room. Recess lighting here is used to display a conversation area.

Track lighting can be used on walls as well as on ceiling.

Glamorous Curtain Walls

If the end wall of that part of the room has some ugly windows that are hard to decorate, or perhaps no windows at all, create a "glamour" wall by running a drape clear across the room. Install fluorescent lamps inside the cornice above the drape, so they shine down on it. You also could use a dimmer switch with incandescent lamps.

Some types of fluorescents can be controlled by dimmer switches, but they are a special type and somewhat more expensive than standard lamps.

For a really special effect, if the drapes are white, use colored lamps or colored filters so the lights make the draped wall a mass of color. You can change the colors to suit your mood, or the feeling you want to create for a particular get-together.

Save Energy...
Add A Skylight

1. *Allow yourself 2 to 4 hours of clear weather for the job. To install Skymaster low-profile skylight, which fits cleanly in with shingles and has no curb, drive 3-in. nail up through the roof at the four corners marking the location of your skylight. Be sure there are no electrical wires, pipes or ducts in the way.*

3. *Frame the opening, top and bottom. Rafters will form the sides of the framing. If you are using a bigger skylight and rafter runs through the opening, cut the rafter back to make room for the new framing.*

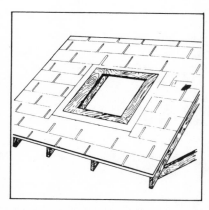

2. *Go up on the roof, locate the nails protruding through, and remove roofing material back about 12 inches around the area. Cut hole through the roof decking.*

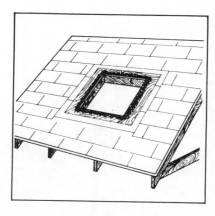

4. *Apply roofing mastic around the opening about ¼-inches thick, covering all exposed wood and felt. Use a black roofing mastic such as GAF, Johns-Manville, Bird & Son, or similar.*

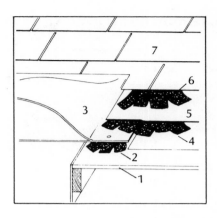

5. *Position skylight over the opening. Drill small holes for the nails. Nail each corner down in line with the rafter, with a 6d or 8d nail. Use ¾-inch rustproof roofing nails around the flange, about 3 inches apart.*

8. *This drawing shows the sequence of materials: 1, roof deck; 2, mastic; 3, skylight; 4, mastic; 5, roofing felt; 6, mastic; 7, shingles.*

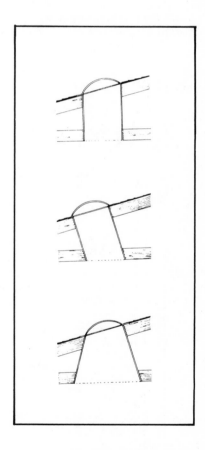

6. *Apply mastic over the edge of skylight right up to the bubble. Cut strips of roofing felt wide enough to go from the bubble to overlap the felt on the deck. Apply more mastic over these strips at the top and apply the top strip of felt. Don't put a strip on the bottom.*

9. *If you want to make a light shaft you can angle it to direct the sunlight. Straight down is best, but if there is some obstruction you can avoid it by angling the shaft. You also might want to make the bottom of the shaft bigger to distribute the light over a broader area. You can use ¼-inch plywood or hardboard for the shaft, paint the inside white, leave the bottom open or cut a plastic diffuser to cover it.*

7. *Apply mastic over the felt strips and replace shingles. After shingles are in place, apply mastic across the bottom of the skylight.*

ALTERNATIVE: THE CURB MODEL

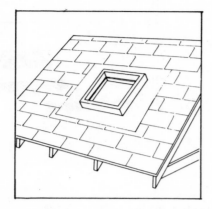

5. *For a curb-type skylight, steps 1 through 4 are the same as for low-profile model. (See preceding pages). Then construct the curb with 2x6 lumber. This will go on top of the roof deck, so inside dimensions of curb will be same as the opening. Be sure to use mastic in all joints.*

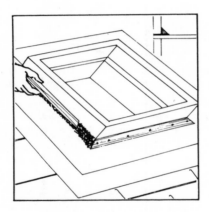

6. *Apply mastic on the outside of the curb at the bottom, and nail cant strips in place. These are triangular moldings that will hold the curb in place.*

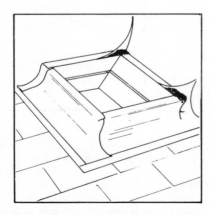

7. *Cover entire outside of curb with mastic, then cover with strips of roofing felt. First put on the bottom one, then the sides, then the top. Be sure to apply mastic everywhere the felt overlaps, and cover all exposed seams with mastic.*

8. *Replace shingles.*

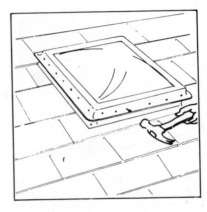

9. *Apply a bead of clear mastic around the top edge of the curb and press skylight down into place. Drill small holes for nails or screws and secure flange around edge about every 3 inches.*

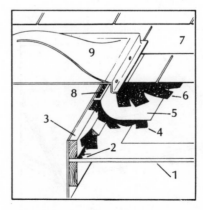

10. *Sequence here is: 1, roof deck; 2, mastic; 3, curb; 4, mastic; 5, roofing felt; 6, mastic; 7, shingles; 8, clear mastic; 9, skylight.*

5. Build A Bar

Although bars are generally considered a part of a family room, recreation room or the kitchen, they can also do duty in the living room for entertaining away from the rest of the family. Or they can do double duty by providing a divider between two rooms.

Building Wet or Dry Bars

If there is enough room for a wet bar, and you are not afraid to do some rudimentary plumbing, it can be built in a corner of the room, on one wall, even in the wall. Flexible or rigid plastic piping permits running water up through a wall or floor where rigid metal pipe would be impractical to install. Some pipe and fittings can be simply joined with adhesive, other types use clamps much like hose clamps. Drains can be installed with plastic materials also.

Where water and drain lines would not be practical, as in a room on a concrete slab, you'll have to settle for a dry setup.

The bar itself can be a simple framework of 1 x 2's or 2 x 4's covered with paneling matching that used on the wall. To make it even more practical—if it's a dry bar—a set of heavy-duty casters underneath will permit rolling the bar against the wall where it will do duty as a serving counter when not being used for dispensing beverages.

Where space is really a problem, you can build a bar right into the wall. For simple construction, remove the wallboard or paneling to create a recess in the wall between the studs. Install shelves, perhaps mirror tile behind the shelves. Extend the shelves a bit and build a "shadow box" picture frame that projects 2 or 3 inches from the wall. It covers the bar when not in use, drops down to be a counter when needed.

Shown on page 63 is one method of utilizing a bar and "pass through" from a kitchen dining area to the living room. This project was undertaken in an old farm house. The bar is on the kitchen side. Bar stools on the "living room" side provide a space for conversation and allow guests to visit with the host and hostess when a meal is being prepared.

Although your particular house and situation may be a little bit different, you might be interested in applying some of the techniques used in remodeling and redecorating the old house shown. By the use of rough-sawn white cedar as trim, and simulated bricks for covering the wall and the old flue, as well as a cedar-shingled soffit concealing over-counter lights and a countertop

Although often considered only for dining rooms or recreation rooms, bars can also be an integral part of a living room if care is taken to insure the bar fits the general decorating scheme.

Although elegant, bar can be as simple as a "wine rack" and a place to store glasses and a carafe of wine.

Even a small folding table can occasionally do duty as a bar.

Corner bar has suspended panel lighted ceiling under dropped ceiling. Note the unique wine storage rack built above bar.

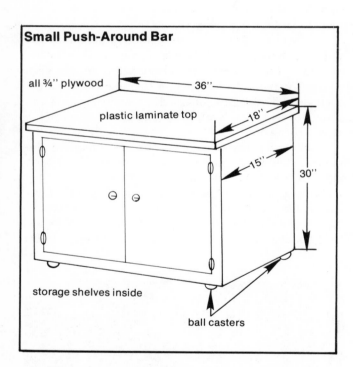

Small Push-Around Bar

all ¾'' plywood

36''

plastic laminate top

18''

15''

30''

storage shelves inside

ball casters

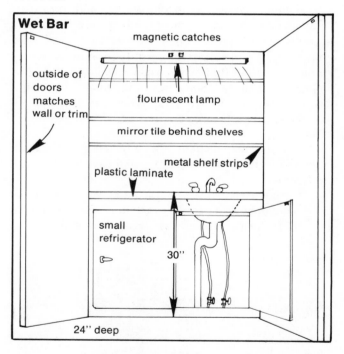

Wet Bar

magnetic catches

outside of doors matches wall or trim

flourescent lamp

mirror tile behind shelves

metal shelf strips

plastic laminate

small refrigerator

30''

24'' deep

bar, the redecorated wall of the dining area became a real conversation wall. It has the elegance, charm and warmth of an authentic brick wall in an old building.

Construction

The first step was to cut the opening. Because the wall shown was a non-load-bearing wall, cutting the opening wasn't much of a problem, nor was framing in the opening. If at all possible, the easiest method of cut-ting an opening and framing it is by locating the opening so one or more of the sides will be framed by an existing stud. A lot of planning at this stage can save a lot of work later on. Measure the proposed opening, locate the existing studs and mark the proposed location temporarily on the wall. By adjusting the size of the opening, you may be able to get in between existing studs, and your job will be much easier. If you can't fit the opening between existing studs, the framing still won't be hard with a non-load-bearing wall, but it will be a bit harder on a load-bearing wall. To determine which type wall you're working on,

Left: *Opening in wall opens kitchen to rest of house and makes both rooms more practical. Recessed lights in the overhead soffit provide subtle lighting and accentuate brick wall.*
Right: *Kitchen side of opening is as attractive as living room side.*

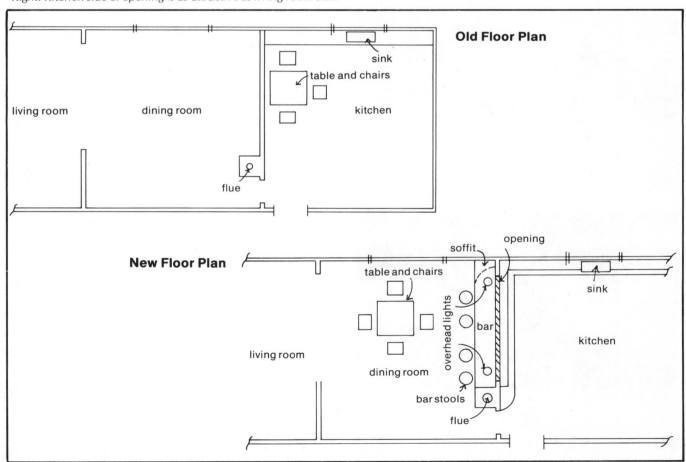

Kitchen was completely shut off from rest of house by wall between living room and kitchen. (Shown after stripping, but before cutting.)

First step is to locate opening and mark outline on both sides of wall. Remove plaster with chisel then cut away laths.

Cut away studs starting at top, then cutting away bottom.

go up in the attic and see if the ceiling joists cross the wall at right angles. If they do, the wall is supporting the ceiling and is called a load-bearing wall. Naturally if it is an outside wall, it will be a load-bearing wall. If the ceiling joists run parallel to the wall, it is a non-load-bearing wall.

After determining the exact location of the opening, mark it on the wall using a crayon and a straightedge. First, use an old, wide chisel to cut away the plaster along the lines, then use a hammer to knock out the plaster between the lines. Repeat this procedure on the opposite side of the wall. With all the plaster removed, use the chisel to cut away a couple of laths on each side of the wall until you can get a hand saw in place, then cut away the remaining laths with the hand saw. With the plaster and laths removed, you can turn the handsaw down flat and cut away the studs left in the opening. If you're working on a load-bearing wall, you'll have to cut away the plaster and laths clear to the floor where the ends of the opening will be so you can install the side-support framing members.

The type of framing you install in the opening will depend on whether the wall is non-load-bearing or load-bearing. Figures 5.1 and 5.2 illustrate the proper methods of framing both types of wall. The main difference is that if the wall is non-load-bearing, the best method is to simply assemble the frame, then slide the assembled frame in the opening and nail it in place.

The framing for a load-bearing wall must, however, support not only the wall, but the overhead joists, etc., as well. The framing for a load-bearing wall must be supported by 2 x 4's that run all the way down to the floor sill plate. There must be two at each end, or you can ''scab'' or nail on a 2 x 4 to an existing stud if it is in the right place. The top portion of the framing is made out of 2-bys placed on edge and nailed together. Normally, if the distance across the opening is no more than 6 feet, you can use 2 x 4's. If the opening will mean removing more than two or three studs, you should use 2 x 6's. Also on outside walls, and other walls carrying more weight than ceiling joists alone, you should also use 2 x 6's or larger for the top support beam. To help space out the 2-bys in the top support, use laths as spacers between them. Make sure the frame is square and securely fastened in place in the opening. If you're going to be installing sheet rock or paneling over the old wall, you will have to add spacers on each side of the framing to equal the depth of the old plaster and laths that have been chiseled away. Tack these in place and install the new wall board or paneling as desired.

In the remodeling job shown, the next step was to build the countertop as shown in Figures No. 5.3, 5.4, 5.5. This was completely assembled, then fastened to the wall as shown. The countertop was supported on the din-

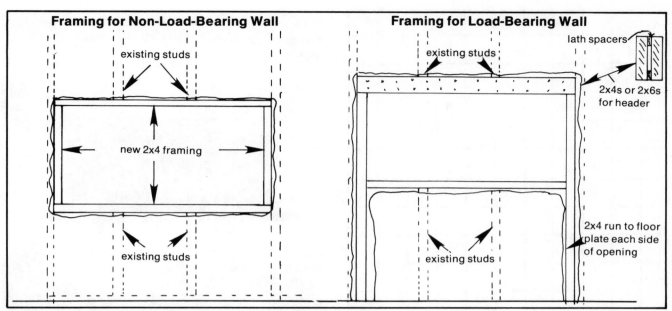

Fig. 5.1. Framing for non-load-bearing wall.

Fig. 5.2. Framing for load-bearing wall.

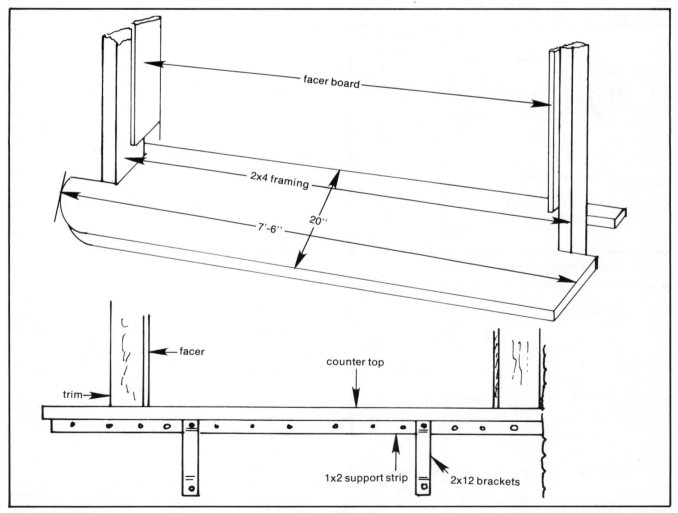

Fig. 5.3   Shelf

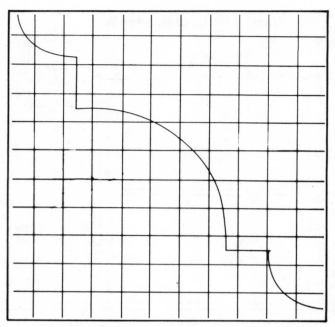

Fig. 5.4   *Squared drawing of countertop brackets.*

The countertop and the soffit frame have been assembled and fastened to the wall.

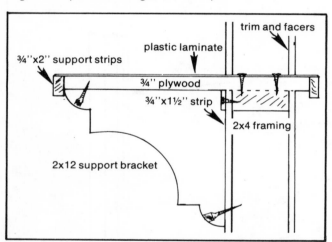

Fig. 5.5   *Detail-side view of countertop and brackets.*

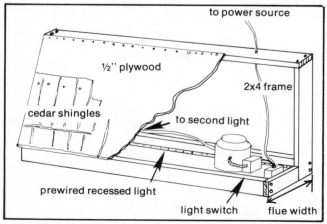

Fig. 5.6   *Overhead light soffit.*

ing room side by 2 x 12 braces that were cut in a fancy motif. Because the old flue stuck out in the room, and was still usable, we decided to utilize it and build around it. The countertop was made so it would fit flush with the outside edge of the chimney.

After building and installing the countertop, the next step was to build and install the overhead light soffit. It also was made to fit in flush with the front edge of the old flue. Recessed ceiling boxes were installed in the soffit as shown in Figure No. 5.6, and a switch installed on one end of the soffit for turning them off and on.

Decoration

With the hard part of the work done, the next step was to start the redecorating. Two items were utilized to give the wall its unusual look. Rough-sawn white cedar was given a coat of stain-sealer and installed as trim around the opening and at the ends and top and bottom of the wall. The trim was made of wide boards to leave the impression of beams left in the wall. By filling in the openings left between the trim boards with simulated ''used-brick,'' the entire wall looks like the beams and bricks of an old building.

The simulated bricks are fiberglass and made in sheets that overlap each other much like the finger-laps in a wooden joint. Installing sheets like this is much faster

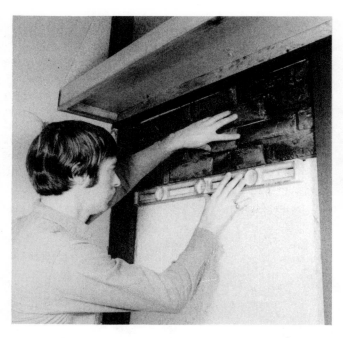

One of the features that gives the room real charm is the "brick" wall. The bricks are actually fiberglass panels that simulate the look of old "used bricks." First step is to cut panels to size and level them up for the first row.

After determining position of brick sheet, the backside is coated with panel adhesive using a caulking gun and panel is installed on wall. Tiny flat head nails are driven in to help hold bricks to wall.

than installing the single bricks. The sheets of bricks may be fastened to the wall with either panel adhesive or small flat-head nails driven through holes punched or drilled through the fiberglass in the recessed "joint" areas between the bricks. Because the panels were to be installed on an old wall with peeling wallpaper and loose plaster, I decided to use both methods, and nail and glue the panels in place.

The first step is to start the first panel and make sure it is level and square with the corner of the wall or trim as shown. Punch or drill the holes for the nails, then using panel adhesive in caulking gun, run a line of adhesive on the back protruding edges of the panel. Position the panel in place and drive the nails in place. You will have to recess the nails back in the joints by using a nail set. After installing the first sheet, install the next one, fitting the bricks in place so the joints between the bricks are nice and even. Continue installing the bricks until the wall is finished.

The fiberglass brick panels may be cut with a hacksaw, but one fast and easy method I found for cutting them was to use an old, dull plywood blade in my radial arm saw. The old saw blade, without any set in it, literally burned its way through fast and made a smooth, nice cut.

Inside corners are made by merely butting the bricks against each other in the corner. The outside corners are made by using special L-shaped outside corner panels

Second layer of brick panels is installed. Note how panel is made so next panel will fit into it. Nail heads are set back in brick joints using a nail set.

that simulate the stacking of bricks on a corner. In our case, these panels were used to cover the old flue. After installing both corners of the flue with corner panels, individual bricks were cut to fit between the two outside panels. The bricks shown may also be easily snapped apart from the panel and installed as individual bricks, in case you wish to simulate an arched doorway or some other such unusual manner of bricklaying.

After cutting and installing all bricks, the next step is to add the "mortar" to the wall. The mortar for the bricks is actually a sand-filled material applied by the caulking gun. It is simply squeezed into the joints formed between the bricks in the panels, and between the panels. By using the tip of your finger you can easily spread the "mortar" around and even out the joints, making them appear even more realistic. The main trick in applying the mortar material properly is to have it heated. I found the best method was to run the sink full of hot water and drop the tubes into the sink. After about ten minutes the material had become warm and soft enough to easily work with the

Process is continued down wall.

There are also panels of bricks which simulate outside corner bricks, and these were used around old plastered flue.

After installing both corner panels, bricks were cut to length and fitted between to finish the job.

What gives the brick wall that extreme realism is the use of the special "mortar." It has sand in it and when dried looks exactly like mortar. First step is to place tube of mortar in hot water, to allow it to become soft, then apply with caulking gun.

caulking gun. When it dries, it becomes hard and sandy and really resembles the real thing.

With the brick wall finished, the next step was to install the cedar shingles on the overhead soffit. Begin by laying a single course along the edge of the soffit. Then lay a second course directly over the top of this, but overlapping so none of the plywood cover of the soffit is showing. Then measure up about 7 inches and start the next course of shingles. As shown in photo at right, you can use a small square for measuring, or snap a chalkline on the shingles. Continue laying courses until the ceiling is reached, then cut the last course to fit in place.

Now the room is ready for carpet, draperies and all the trimmings. Not only did the remodeled rooms become much more functional, but their appearance matched the look of the rest of the old farm house. (Bricks by Roxite; Lighting fixtures by Thomas Industries).

To install wood shingles to overhead soffit, nail on two rows on the bottom edge, overlapping the first with the second. Then start nailing on the next course, measuring from the bottom edge of the first shingles with a small square.

If you wish you may use the tip of your finger to smooth down the "joint" between the bricks and give it an even more real appearance.

Continue nailing on shingles until you reach the top, then cut the top course to fit.

Create A Corner Bar

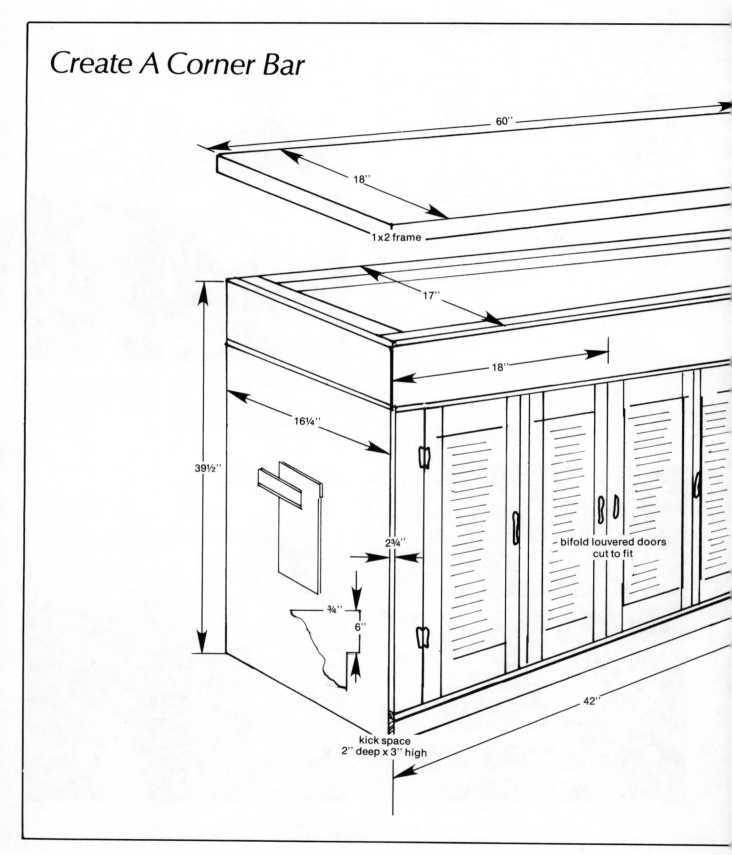

60''

18''

1x2 frame

17''

18''

16¼''

39½''

2¾''

¾''

6''

bifold louvered doors
cut to fit

42''

kick space
2'' deep x 3'' high

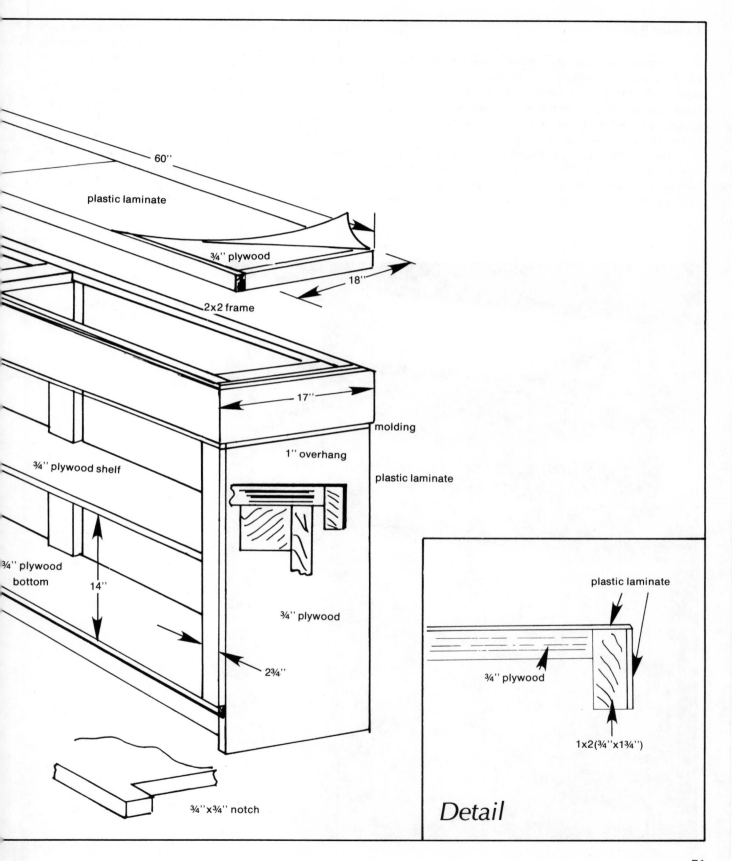

60"

plastic laminate

¾" plywood

2x2 frame

18"

17"

molding

1" overhang

plastic laminate

¾" plywood shelf

¾" plywood

¾" plywood bottom

14"

2¾"

¾"x¾" notch

plastic laminate

¾" plywood

1x2(¾"x1¾")

Detail

Corner Bar

A corner bar can solve many problems. This bar is easily made using only portable electric or even hand tools, except for the countertop which can be purchased ready-made through building supply stores. If you have a router and a radial-arm or table saw, you can easily make the plastic-laminated bar top as well.

The bar framing is constructed of 2 x 2 stock glued and screwed together. Then the ¾ inch fir plywood ends, bottom, shelves and back are fastened in place with glue and finishing nails which are countersunk and the holes filled with wood putty. Purchased louvered doors were installed in place and the bar was painted and antiqued to match the color of the carpeting. The countertop is made as shown on preceding pages and fastened in place with screws from the underside and into the plywood top. The countertop features imitation black slate and matches the rustic look of the room perfectly.

After finishing the cabinet and countertop, metal shelf-support strips were screwed to the wall. Smoky-colored mirror tiles with gold veining were fastened to the wall and glass shelves were cut to fit the shelf brackets. A recessed light fixture was installed over the bar.

A small corner bar can utilize space that would otherwise be wasted. Mirror tile with glass shelves also provides illusion of more space.

Living rooms should make the most of their unusual features--in this case, a lovely setting and a soaring fireplace wall. Track lighting focuses on large painting, and raised built-in seating creates illusion of a conversation pit. (Photo courtesy of California Redwood Association; Architect Carlton Sturges Abbott; James N. Cargill Residence; Taylor Lewis photographer)

A bar can link rooms and functional areas together; this one ties the living area into the kitchen. (For instructions on building this bar, see Chapter 5.)

One way to create an entertainment center is to have a complete home entertainment center installed; shown is a package by NuTone with intercom, plus music and additional features.

Factory-made kitchen cabinets are now being used in every room of the home. A whole wall or any part of it can be used, and in an apartment it can be free-standing for moving. This couple has used lumber for open shelving, and around it they are fitting Boise Cascade's Olde Dominion cabinets. The cabinets are available in many other styles as well. Exposed edges and sides are then painted in a matching or contrasting color.

Quality textured hardboard paneling offers two-toned effect of real wood; paneling is "Barnside" by Marlite Paneling.

Accent wall of rich brown tile sets off both the warm wood walls and the light ceiling. (Photo courtesy of American Olean Tile Co.) ▶

This bar was converted from a walk-in closet (below) in the hallway next to the living room. The entryway wall adjoined the living room wall into which a hole was cut, exposing the closet. Support studs were removed to create opening; paneling was cut to fit partition framework. Formica bar with padded rail was mounted on the opening with braces. Back bar is formica over top-mounting kitchen cabinets that were placed on floor, and supported by plywood platform 6 inches high. Back bar wall uses alternating strips of mirror squares and paneling cut to form ''V'' that breaks up and reflects the light. Bar-size refrigerator is hidden, as is bathroom behind bar into which plumbing can be tapped for a wet bar (photo by W. McGrath).

This 8-foot bar has a special look, created by two long fluorescent tubes mounted under the "Corian" top. The simulated marble is translucent and transmits a soft light through the ½-inch thickness. This effect also could be created with a number of incandescent bulbs, which could be almost any color.

Raised fireplace can be installed without reinforcing the floor. Free-standing custom hood, combined with low couches, gives illusion of height and space in the room. (Ember Box Fireplaces; photo courtesy of Fireplace Institute)

Four different planes of "Corian" are laminated to create the sculptured look of this fireplace. The simulated marble can be sawed, shaped and routed much like wood, with woodworking tools. This fireplace has a gas log; "Corian" is not recommended for wood-burning fireplaces.

Laminate-covered bar top provides both durability and beauty. (Thomasville Basement; photo courtesy of Masonite Corp.)

An accent panel of Western Wood board paneling sets off
a modern fireplace in this living room that is open on three
sides. (Western Wood Products)

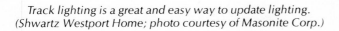

Track lighting is a great and easy way to update lighting.
(Shwartz Westport Home; photo courtesy of Masonite Corp.)

With free-standing fireplace unit, all you need is a special flue
and fire protection on the walls.

A fireplace need not be traditional--it can be as modern and sophisticated as you like.
(Photo courtesy of Marlite)

This Supergraphic creates interest and focuses on the living room area in a one-room apartment. The light, bright colors and the design draw your eye right to the balcony (Wood Davies & Co., Ltd.). Supergraphic packages are available in most decorating stores or home centers.

Use particleboard framing prefabricated metal firebox, and Z-Brick for an elegant and functional fireplace.

Fireplaces can become accent walls themselves. The hearth is an extension of the brick wall, for both easy cleaning and fire protection.

6. Entertainment Centers

Today's living rooms are more than just a room with a few chairs. They are much more versatile, and can provide an "entertainment" room as well as "sitting" room. The focal point of many of these multipurpose living rooms is an entertainment center.

In a contemporary living room, an entertainment center can be just open shelves, purchased or made, with stereo components, and perhaps a television set on them. If the living room is to be used for social events, where a television is an unwelcome noisy "eye," it should be in a cabinet with doors so it can be out of sight when not wanted. Some console models come with doors where the cabinet itself is quite handsome and can even be used as a serving surface.

Where the television set has no doors, it can be fitted in a custom-made cabinet, but provisions for ventilation must be made. Even solid-state sets create considerable heat, which must be eliminated if the set is to work properly and for any length of time. Ventilation can be provided by an opening or grille under the set and one above. Where space is restricted, you can install a small, quiet fan designed for cooling electronic devices.

If your hobby is home movies or making slides a projection screen can be built into your entertainment wall. Generally a narrow, horizontal cabinet will hold a roll-down (or roll-up) projection screen. A small cabinet across the room will provide storage for the projectors and/or slides and movie reels.

Wall of cabinets has framework of 2x4s over which wall paneling is glued and nailed. Note that base is made of vertical 2x4s in U-shape, with other 2x4s positioned flat on top of them. Inner edges of 2x4s are flush, so flat 2x4 creates toe space. Doors of cabinets consist of frames glued and nailed from 1x2s, with paneling glued and bradded to them. Bottom shelf in cabinets is ¾-inch plywood, with remaining shelves also cut from plywood, resting on cleats of 1x2 nailed to 2x4 frame. Open shelves are glass or clear plastic fitted on brackets fitted to metal standards that are screwed to walls of cabinets.

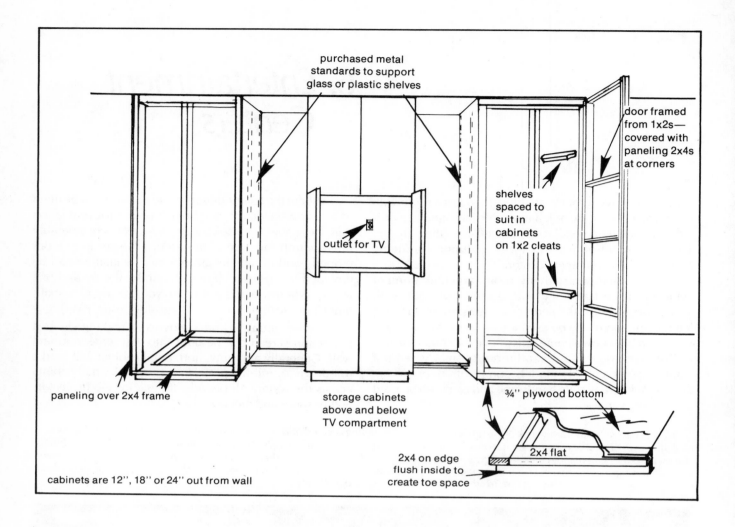

purchased metal
standards to support
glass or plastic shelves

door framed
from 1x2s—
covered with
paneling 2x4s
at corners

outlet for TV

shelves
spaced to
suit in
cabinets
on 1x2 cleats

paneling over 2x4 frame

storage cabinets
above and below
TV compartment

¾'' plywood bottom

2x4 flat

2x4 on edge
flush inside to
create toe space

cabinets are 12'', 18'' or 24'' out from wall

If the projectors have sound capabilities, the same speakers used for your hi-fi might be used for them. There are bookshelf speakers that fit snugly on shelves; some speakers double as small chairside tables. The type you use will depend on space available, and how much you want to spend on them.

An entertainment center needn't stop with a hi-fi set, projector, or television set. For the dedicated model builder or craftsperson, there are desks and even workbenches that are beautiful enough to go into even a living room, providing the workspace needed for a favorite hobby. Or again you can build the unit into a wall and it can be covered with doors when not in use.

In most cases entertainment centers mean cabinets and if you don't have the means to build them yourself, one answer is to purchase unfinished modular cabinet sections and install them. Many of the kitchen cabinets today are as beautiful as furniture, and leading manufac-

An entertainment center can also be quite simple as this work desk/book storage.

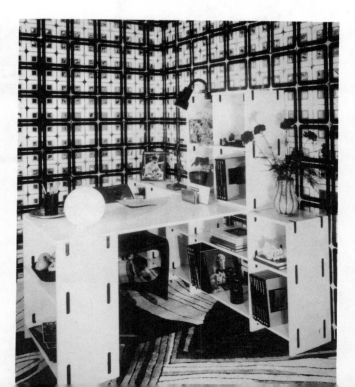

Or your interest may go to the green thumb set. Lighted display shelves show off house plants; storage space underneath with touch latches conceals materials and tools needed for hobby.

turers say people purchasing cabinets for their kitchens are coming back for extra cabinet units for dens, bedrooms, living rooms, you name it. Installation of the units is quite easy and almost anyone with a little hammer and nail experience can do it.

Building A Combination Cabinet-Bookshelf

If on the other hand you wish to build your own cabinets, for instance customizing them to suit existing furniture, you can do that as well, but you will naturally need more tools and experience. The cabinet shown is made much in the same manner as purchased unfinished cabinets; however, when you're building a cabinet yourself you can size it to fit your particular needs. For instance the cabinet shown is made just higher than usual so it will correspond with the chair rail trim around the room.

You can make your own combined cabinet and bookshelf such as this one.

Build A Bookshelf

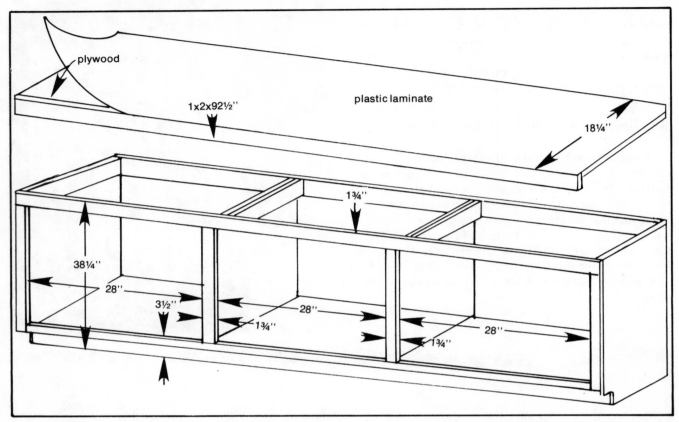

plywood

1x2x92½''

plastic laminate

18¼''

1¾''

38¼''

28''

3½''

1¾''

28''

28''

1¾''

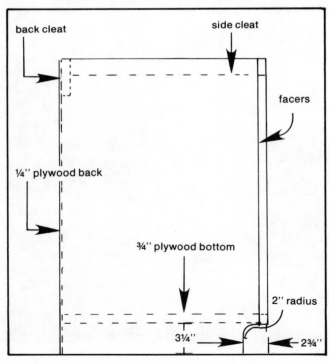

back cleat

side cleat

facers

¼'' plywood back

¾'' plywood bottom

2'' radius

3¼''

2¾''

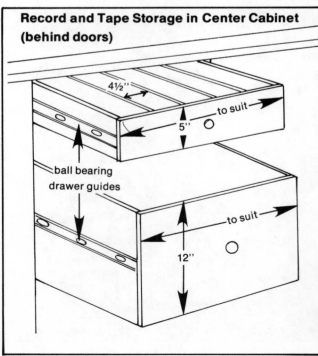

Record and Tape Storage in Center Cabinet (behind doors)

4½''

to suit

5''

ball bearing
drawer guides

to suit

12''

Construction

The first step is to cut all visible side pieces from hardwood, plywood or coreboard. Then cut the interior dividers and non-showing side pieces from ¾ inch fir plywood. Note that the side pieces have a decorative notch cut for the kickboard. This can be cut using a saber saw. Then route a ¼ x ¼ inch rabbet on the inside back edge of each side piece. The inside dividers have a notch cut in them to accept a 1 x 2 on their top back edge. Cut the bottom supports from 2 x 4's and cut the bottom from ¾ plywood and nail it in place on the supports.

Next, nail or screw the side pieces in place. Turn the cabinet unit over on its front and nail and glue the back 1 x 2 top support in place. Turn the cabinet over again on its back.

Cut a ¼ inch plywood back, making sure it is cut square and then fit it in place in the rabbets on the sides and square up the cabinet to fit, then nail and glue it in place. This insures that the cabinet will be square and makes the rest of the construction much easier.

Cut the 1 x 2 facings and glue and nail them in place, fitting each piece individually to insure that they fit properly. Use a nail set to set the nails below the surface of the wooden facers, then fill the holes with wood putty. Use a belt sander to sand all facing surfaces flush, then follow with a finishing sander to remove the sanding marks made by the belt sander.

The shelves inside the cabinet can be held in place utilizing shelf bracket strips, or by nailing shelf cleats in the positions you wish the shelves to be.

Stain and finish the cabinet to suit.

First step is to cut side and divider sections from plywood.

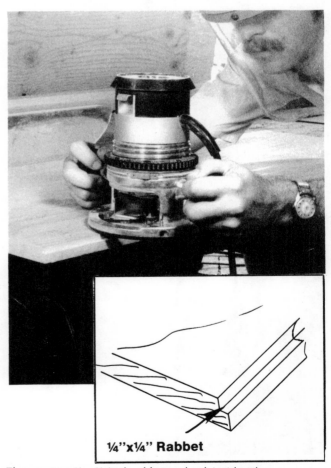

¼"x¼" Rabbet

Then route a ¼ x ¼ inch rabbet on back inside edges.

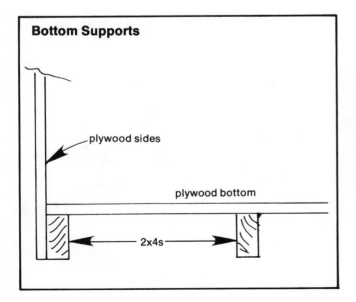

Bottom Supports

plywood sides

plywood bottom

2x4s

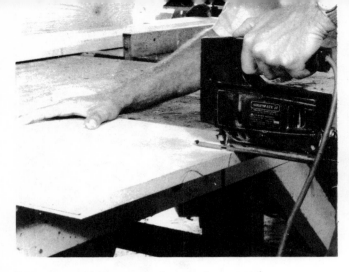

Cut away toe kick space notch on each open end.

Turn cabinet over on back and nail and glue on front facers.

Cut notches in back top of dividers, nail cabinet together. Back support strip is being nailed in place here.

Use nail set to set finishing nails below wood surface.

Nail on ¼ inch plywood back to square up cabinet.

Fill nail holes and open wood joints with wood putty.

Use belt sander to rough sand all surfaces, then finishing sander to smooth away marks by belt sander.

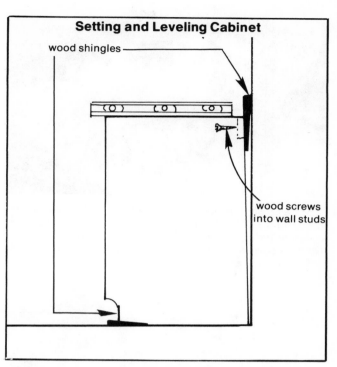

Setting and Leveling Cabinet

wood shingles

wood screws into wall studs

Stain and finish to suit, then install cabinet in place.

Installation

You can install the doors first, or set the cabinet at this time and make the doors, then install them. To set the cabinet, place it in position against the wall and use a level to level it up. Wooden shingles can be used as shims to bring the cabinet up to level. They can also be used behind the cabinet in places where the wall may curve away from the cabinet back. When the cabinet is leveled entirely, nail it in place to the studs in the wall, through the back and the top back 1 x 2. If it fits against an end wall, nail through the end as well.

Doors

The doors are made of ¾ inch hardwood faced plywood or coreboard, and are cut ⅜ inch larger on top, bottom and one side for double doors. They are cut ⅜ inch larger all around for single doors. When all doors have been cut to size, route or cut a ⅜ inch by ⅜ inch rabbet on those sides. Note on single doors the ⅜ inch rabbet will extend around the entire door.

The decorative front on the doors shown was cut using a ¼ inch veiner bit and a router. The pattern was cut using a Wing template. The template is adjusted to place the pattern in the correct position on the doors, then merely pushed around the doors and locked in place. The

Install doors on cabinet and place magnetic catches to hold doors shut.

Make up plywood top with 1 x 1¾ inch banding around exposed sides. Coat both plastic laminate front and side strips with adhesive and glue in place. Use belt sander to cut away excess laminate down to wood surface and to smooth down top of wood surface.

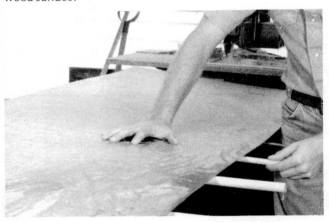

Coat wooden surface and plastic laminate top piece with adhesive. Use wood dowels or strips to prevent top from touching wood until you have it positioned exactly. Then pull out strips and use pressure on laminate top to firm it down onto wood surface.

Plastic laminate trimmer used in router is used to cut away excess laminate and finish edge.

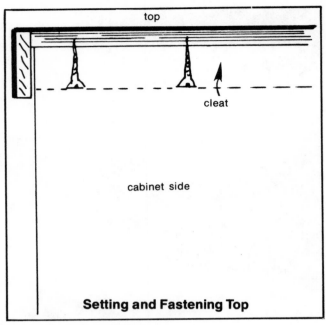

Setting and Fastening Top

Top is installed on cabinet.

router is then placed in the template and used to cut the pattern. Depending on the corner patterns used with the template, a variety of patterns can be routed on the doors. When the doors have been cut and routed, sand thoroughly and stain and varnish to match the cabinet. Then install ⅜ inch overlap hinges and the desired knobs. Position the doors in place and install in the cabinet.

Cabinet Top

Now to install the top. The top shown is made of plastic laminate, which can be cleaned easily with a damp cloth; the simulated black slate adds elegance to the room. The first step is to cut a ¾ inch fir plywood piece the same size as the top of the cabinet. Then nail a 1 x 2 wood strip around all exposed edges. Position the top in place to check for fit. Then cut a piece of laminate for each side strip using a radial arm saw with an old plywood blade, or router, or saber saw. If using saber saw, clamp laminate down to a solid surface so it won't chatter.

Using laminate adhesive, coat both the laminate and the wooden surface and allow to dry thoroughly. Then stick the laminate to the wooden surface. Once you put it down you can't move it, so if the strip is a long one, you'll need an extra hand to place it accurately.

With the laminate strips securely in place, use a belt sander to smooth them down flush with the top surface and to even out the entire front edge where the wood strip joins the plywood top. Coat the top piece of laminate and the top of the wood surface and allow to dry. Place

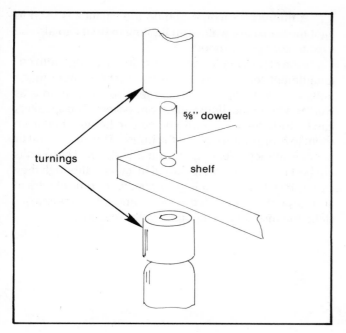

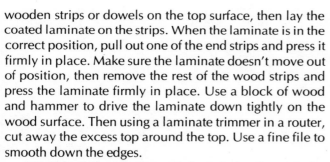

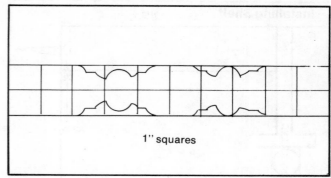

1" squares

wooden strips or dowels on the top surface, then lay the coated laminate on the strips. When the laminate is in the correct position, pull out one of the end strips and press it firmly in place. Make sure the laminate doesn't move out of position, then remove the rest of the wood strips and press the laminate firmly in place. Use a block of wood and hammer to drive the laminate down tightly on the wood surface. Then using a laminate trimmer in a router, cut away the excess top around the top. Use a fine file to smooth down the edges.

To install the top, bore ¼ inch holes through the back edge and interior cleats. Place top in position making sure it fits the wall properly. If not, you can use a belt sander to cut away any excess top, or later use a trim strip to cover any gaps between wall and top. Then screw top in place from underside of top cleats of cabinet using No. 10 x 2¼ inch screws.

You can make the bookcase supports using purchased turnings, or turn your own to suit. In any case the turnings are fitted with threaded wooden dowels, or plain dowels if you wish to turn them yourself, fitted through the shelves.

The top valance board is cut to shape using a saber saw, then support cleats are screwed to its back edge. There are holes bored through the valance cleats, through which toggle bolts are used to fasten the valance to the ceiling. Measure carefully between cabinet top and ceiling and make the entire valance and bookcase section as one piece, then place it on the cabinet and secure it in place. The bottom of the turning supports are held to the cabinet with wooden dowels.

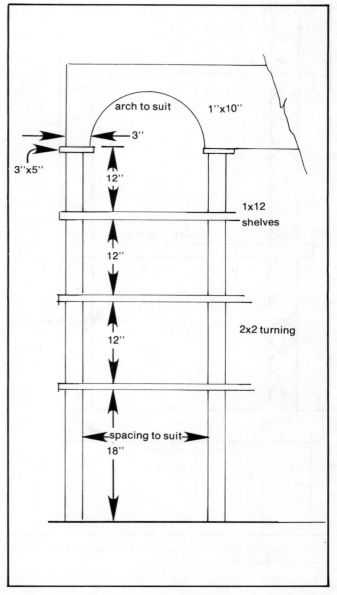

Shelves and turnings are held in place with wooden dowels or threaded wooden rods.

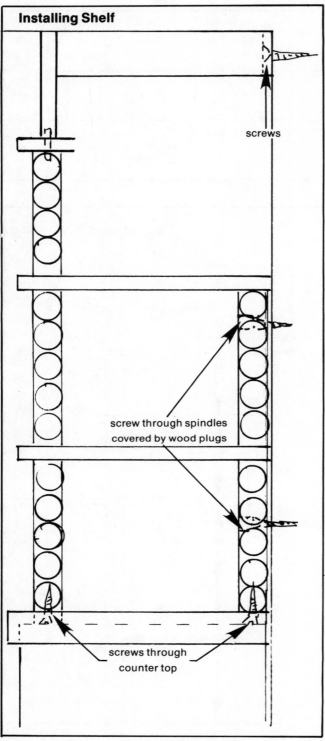

Installing Shelf

screws

screw through spindles
covered by wood plugs

screws through
counter top

Shelf unit with top board is installed as one piece and fastened to wall and cabinet.

A fluorescent fixture behind the valance is used to light the bookcase wall. Strip lighting in front can also be used to change the mood.

One of the simpler ways to achieve a living room entertainment center is to purchase one of the custom-made units such as by NuTone. These feature full hi-fi units as well as a complete house intercom system. The speakers can be installed in each room and can be switched from room to room or throughout the house. The master unit or panel is attractive enough to suit any decor. These units are best installed by professional installers, although they can be installed by a do-it-yourselfer with some electrical and carpentry knowledge—they come with complete installation instructions (photo in color section).

7. Room Dividers

Room dividers are especially good when a living room must serve more than one function, as when one end or corner is used for dining or for a bar.

Many Choices

If the living room is large, you can build a solid room divider so the room is two separate areas, each with a different function. The divider then can be a storage wall, or house a bar, or even a spare closet to take care of your guests' coats.

Alternately, the divider can be just the suggestion of a wall; a see-through grille or a framework supporting a thin-slat blind that can be opened or closed, or even raised up out of the way.

Screens

Time and money, as well as room size and function, will determine the kind of room divider you build. For not too much money you can buy decorator screens that are made of polystyrene plastic, in several different patterns. The screens come with steel tension poles that adjust to fit most ceilings, and hold the screens firmly in place. Because the poles are spring-loaded the screens are not permanently fixed in place; they can be moved to various parts of the living room, or even removed completely and stored away when you need the living room as one large room.

Do you like to shop in second-hand stores, or frequent auctions where furniture is sold? Next time you see old-fashioned Victorian two-, three-, or four-paneled screens that consist of spindles and turnings, buy one if the price is right. Take it home, strip off the old finish and refinish it. You can use stain and varnish if the wood is good, or paint it black, white or even a vivid color.

These screens look good, provide a sense of division in a room, and are readily moved; they can even be placed against a wall out of the way when necessary.

For a room divider that is solid, but which allows light to pass, consider a simple framework to which

This large space needed an open storage wall to serve as a division between seating and the game table area. (Chromcraft furniture)

pieces of translucent fiberglass panels are attached. This kind of screen is much like the oriental "shoji" screen, and would add a nice touch if you wanted a far-east decor in one part of the living room.

Storage

Storage might be your prime reason for a room divider. You can incorporate shelves and cabinets in the divider, and the assembly can be as simple as a counter with shelves or cabinets under it, on to a floor-to-ceiling wall with all kinds of storage.

Or, where the living room is of generous size, but you are short of clothes closets, simply frame in the wall to be a closet. Set the 2 x 4s edgewise to save room, then cover these "studs" with paneling used in the rest of the room, or use plasterboard.

Decorator screens of polystyrene plastic in several colors are fitted with spring-loaded poles that permit easy location at any place in the living room. They also are readily removed for cleaning or relocation. (Photo courtesy Marlite Div. Masonite Corporation)

Old-fashioned panel screen of grille and spindles is "portable" room divider, can be positioned to suit whatever function room is to accommodate. (Photo courtesy Ozite Corporation)

You also can make your own folding screens. Make frames of 1 x 2 lumber flat, nail and glue sheets of ⅛-inch hardboard to both surfaces, then cover with material to suit. Here screens are covered with wallpaper that matches pattern on walls. (Photo courtesy Plexite Industries)

"Shoji" screen is made of black-painted lumber that has translucent plastic fitted in openings. This allows light to pass through, but gives definite sense of division. (Photo courtesy Selig Manufacturing Co.)

Room divider is assembled from unfinished shelf units and cabinets simply screwed or bolted together, then painted suitable color. Cabinet doors could be covered with paneling to match walls.

If you are short of closet space, room divider can provide handy clothes closet to handle coats of your guests, or just be a fine storage space for clothes and off-season bedding for the family. (Photo courtesy Masonite Corporation)

Kitchen cabinets, either wall-hung or base units, can be used to make room divider in living room. Styling of cabinets can be changed by designs on doors and drawer fronts. Stain or paint cabinets to suit your living room decor. (Photo courtesy Excel Wood Products)

Build a Storage Wall Divider

If you have some experience at woodworking, you can build the storage wall/room divider from plywood. A shortcut for the job is to use ready-built cabinets. While you ordinarily think of cabinets as belonging in a kitchen, modern styles run the gamut from plain to Mediterranean to Early-American to very modern. The styling changes in the cabinets are created by the designs of the doors and drawers of the cabinets. All the basic cabinets are the same, being just boxes. Base cabinets will consist of a front panel that includes a door and a drawer front. Wall-hung cabinets will be a door only. If you have the space, the base cabinets are deeper front to back, generally measuring about 24 inches. Wall-hung cabinets are about 18 inches deep. The wall-hung units can be set on frames made from 2 x 4s to provide a toe space (kick space). The backs of either type cabinet will be plain plywood, usually, and some wall-hung cabinets may even be backless.

Cover the open or plain-wood backs with the paneling used in the other part of the living room, or apply wallcovering material to make the back surface of the cabinet room divider an accent wall.

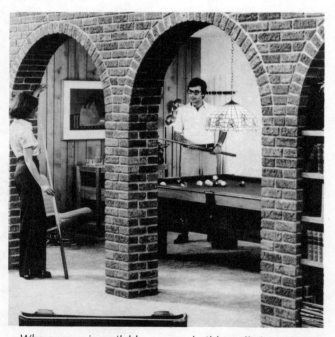

Where space is available, you can build a wall of 2 x 4 framing and cover it with plywood or hardboard. It can be an accent wall as well as a room divider if you cover it with simulated brick or other masonry, or paneling or strongly patterned wallpaper. (Photo courtesy Z-Brick Company)

A

B

(A) If back of arched opening is closed with plywood and covered with simulated masonry or other wallcovering, space can be used for handy book case.
(B) Decorative Franklin stove or prefab fireplace is another option for arched recess in divider wall; unless fire precautions are taken, these should be for show, rather than use.
(C) A couple of shelves and roll-around cart make a handy, compact bar in arched opening, and take up minimum of floor space.
(D) If you have an indoor barbecue in conjunction with the fireplace, arched recess would make fine place for storing pots, pans and utensils. (Photos courtesy Z-Brick Company)

C

D

Building An Arched Room Divider

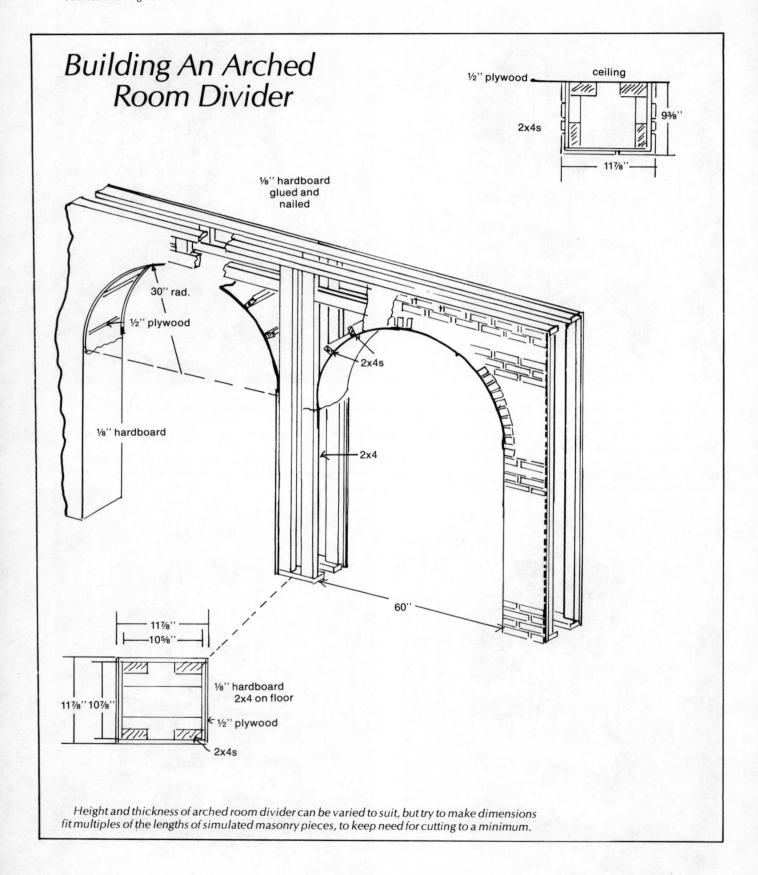

½'' plywood

ceiling

2x4s

9⅜''

11⅞''

⅛'' hardboard
glued and
nailed

30'' rad.

½'' plywood

⅛'' hardboard

2x4s

2x4

60''

11⅞''

10⅝''

11⅞'' 10⅞''

⅛'' hardboard
2x4 on floor

½'' plywood

2x4s

Height and thickness of arched room divider can be varied to suit, but try to make dimensions fit multiples of the lengths of simulated masonry pieces, to keep need for cutting to a minimum.

Construction of wall with arched openings is basic carpentry utilizing 2 x 4s and plywood. Height and thickness of wall is optional, of course, depending on available space.

Curved surfaces inside arches are covered with ⅛-inch hardboard, as it bends readily to a curve, has smooth surface to accept paint, paper or simulated masonry.

Short lengths of 2 x 4 are cut to be snug fit between plywood surfaces of the wall, are nailed in place with finishing nails.

Simulated masonry is applied with mastic that is troweled on plywood and hardboard. Masonry pieces are easily cut with a hacksaw to fit short and angled spaces. (Photos courtesy Z-Brick Company)

Shelves of plywood are combined with ready-built cabinets to create both a room divider and wall storage on outside wall that incorporates additional insulation for energy saving. (Photo courtesy Armstrong Cork Company)

Using Windows

A room divider that is a storage wall can be joined with other storage units on an adjacent wall, and you can even build the shelves and cabinets around a window. The window obviously will be in an exterior wall, and the storage units will add an insulating factor to the wall, and that can be a real plus in this day of energy shortage. It wouldn't be a bad idea to line the backs of the storage units on the outside wall with insulation if your home is an older one that does not have adequate insulation in the walls.

The window itself can be made to add a decorator touch to the living room by framing it in and building a seat that gives additional storage as well as an extra seat. The use of a thin-slat blind can add a touch of color and pattern and also provides an additional seal against heat or cold.

Small-Scale Alternatives

Where you want to set off just one corner of the living room, either for a quiet place for reading or music appreciation, or as a spot for a bar, consider a simple L-shape wall that will stand by itself. The wall is framed with 2 x 4s on edge, then covered with paneling. The wall shown utilizes regular hardboard paneling, but applied diagonally. An added touch is strips of the same paneling applied vertically, as well as across the top and bottom. Note that the wall does not have to be ceiling height. This assures the movement of heated or cooled air, with the wall acting as a baffle against sound and light.

If the plain-wall side of a room divider needs some kind of decoration to keep it from being just a blank surface, consider the thin strips of red cedar that now are available. You can cut the 1/9-inch wood with scissors and glue the pieces to almost any surface with panel adhesive. You can cover the whole wall with any kind of abstract pattern you wish, or create sunbursts or other designs that suit your mood or room decor.

Storage and window seat are provided by simple structure of plywood and hardboard. This is a "Persian" motif, but you can create any kind of styling you wish by applying different designs—even covering surfaces with wallpaper. (Photo courtesy Levolor® Lorentzen)

Simple L-shaped wall is assembled from 2 x 4s on edge, covered with hardboard paneling. Paneling can match that used on other walls, or can be different to provide accent wall. (Photo courtesy Marlite Div. Masonite Corporation)

Window is "boxed in" to provide setting for thin-slat blind, storage and seat is provided by box under the window. Sheets of plywood and/or hardboard (depending on size of window) are framed with 2 x 2s or 2 x 4s.

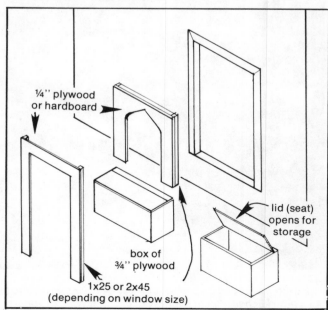

99

For back of L-shape assembly, or any wall that could use decorative accent, strips of cedar ¹/₉-inch thick can be arranged in any pattern that strikes your fancy. Thin wood is cut with ordinary scissors, applied to wall with construction or panel adhesive. *(Photo courtesy Pope and Talbot "Cedarstrip")*

Ready-made room divider that can be slid aside when not needed is folding-screen unit suspended from track on ceiling. These devices come in variety of colors, with wood-grain and plain finishes.

Plastic corrugated curtain becomes attractive room divider that separates living/dining room area from kitchen. *(Photo courtesy of Imperial Wallcoverings)*

Another alternative is to make the room divider an accent wall. Apply brick paneling, or simulated single bricks or stones, or apply a strongly patterned wallpaper.

When you would like a room divider but do not have the room—or perhaps the time and money—for a fixed wall, consider the use of wood-slat (or plastic-slat) curtains that are hung from tracks on the ceiling. These attractive devices come with wood-grain finishes, or in earth tones or even vivid colors, depending on your choice of room decor.

The curtains come with full instructions, and installation generally requires just the attaching to the ceiling of the track, or tracks, then slipping the curtain top into the track and locking it in place. You can install such a curtain the full width or length of a room, or just partway. Two of these curtains installed at right angles will partition off a corner of a room, if that would be your choice.

Similar, though usually more expensive than the assembled units just described, is a heavy drape. The hardware is similar in some respects, but considerable hand sewing and fitting of the drape might be required.

Bringing Outdoors Inside

One factor often overlooked when doing interior work or remodeling in a home—including the living room—is the use of materials ordinarily considered only for outside use. One such item is lattice screening or fencing. This usually is recognized only for garden trellises or screens, but also can be used indoors with good effect.

This kind of material makes a fine room divider, through which light and air can pass. If your living room is to have plants in it, be sure to consider lattice materials.

If you want to be really far out, and like flowers the year around, how about building a planter screen divider. This kind of divider is simply a large box in which the soil for the plants is placed, plus a "screen." The assembly can be covered with lightweight simulated brick or stone. With this kind of divider you'll have the feel of summer all winter long.

Not too many of us have the space in our living room—nor the money to do the job, or the time for it—but a fish pond, with perhaps a spraying fountain in it, can be an ultimate dream.

If your family loves plants, this flower box with "screen" might be the kind of room divider you would like. Unit can be disassembled easily; heavy-duty casters permit moving it around room. (Photo courtesy Z-Brick Company)

For a garden-oriented decor, latticework screens and panels ordinarily used outdoors can be employed inside. They give definite break in room, but allow passage of light and air. (Photo courtesy Plexite Industries)

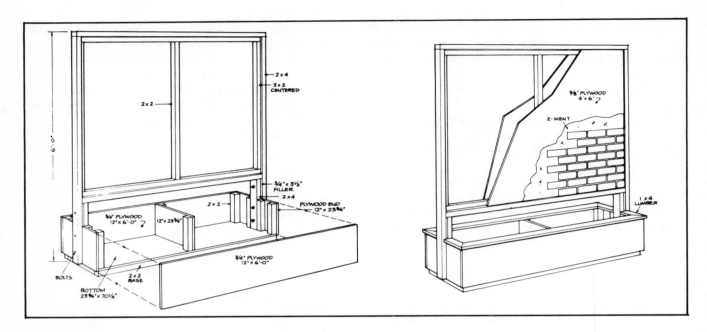

Planter with screen is basically a plywood box with frame above of 2 x 2s and 2 x 4s covered with plywood, over which simulated brick or stone is adhered with adhesive.

If you are going to build a room addition, the pond might be included in the plans. If you need justification, consider that it would provide needed humidity, and the musical sound of falling water has no equal for a soothing caress to your ears.

An open framework around the pond would help to prevent guests from walking into it, and a spotlight would make it highly visible. Swimming fish would be nice, but keep in mind that someone has to feed and tend them. And clean their pool once or twice (or more often) each year. If you want a pond that is beautiful, but has minimum maintenance, better forget the fish.

As with several areas that should have surfaces that require minimum upkeep, ceramic tile would be the answer for the area around the pond.

◄ *If you have a strong architectural feature, such as a fishpond or atrium, you can accent it with an open partition that also serves as a safety divider. Build the frame of 2x4s; a waist-high crosspiece can also be added.*

If you are adding a room to your home, and it will be on a concrete slab, or built over a crawl space, you can include a "conversation pit" like this one. This one is a bit out of the Arabian Nights; it has floors and walls of ceramic tile, with a custom-built fireplace. (Photo courtesy Tile Council of America)

8. Sunken Living Rooms and Conversation Pits

Creating a genuine sunken living room in an existing house would be a major structural change, which would mean the aid of professionals, plus considerable time and money.

Platforms

Since not too many of us have the time, let alone a limitless bank account, the way we achieve a sunken room is to leave the floor right where it is, and build up from it. You then create a "platform" that your guests step up on, before stepping down into your sunken living room.

Height

If you have high ceilings (higher than the standard 8 feet), you can make the platform two or three steps high. If the ceiling is the usual 8-foot height, you can keep the platform just a few inches high, with perhaps a framework of 2 x 4s on edge, covered with plywood or particleboard.

Location

If the platform is built inside the door to the living room, there are some pitfalls to be considered: if you begin the steps up to the platform outside the door, the moment you put your foot on the first step the doorway will be too low. Standard door height is 6 feet 8 inches. Risers (the vertical part of the steps) run from 6 to 8 inches for a normal step, which means that when you stand on the first step the door is 6 feet high or less. People 6 feet tall or over will bump their heads.

If you must build the steps outside the room, then open the wall and raise the height of the door. For a quite dramatic look, open the door clear to the ceiling. You can buy—usually on special order—doors of standard width that are floor-to-ceiling height, should you want a door on the opening.

You can avoid the need for raising the height of the door opening by building the platform inside the room, with the steps up to it in a sort of "well." The height of the ceiling will determine how high the platform can be built: for a standard 8-foot ceiling the maximum platform can

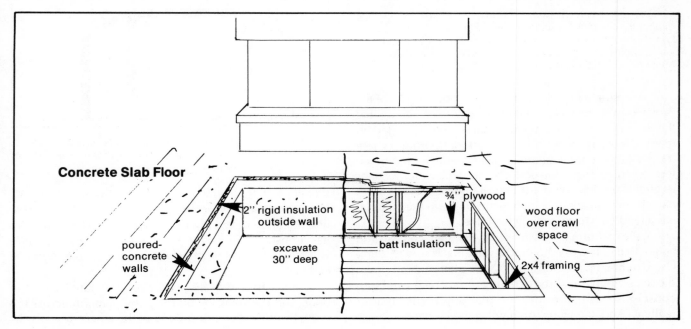

Concrete Slab Floor

2" rigid insulation outside wall

poured-concrete walls

excavate 30" deep

batt insulation

¾" plywood

wood floor over crawl space

2x4 framing

be only 8 to 12 inches; for a cathedral ceiling (can be as high as twelve feet—sometimes higher) build it two or three steps high.

Construction

To build the platform, first remove any carpeting, trim and molding in the area, then assemble the flooring of 2-inch lumber. If your home is built over a crawl space, and the floors are not as warm as they should be, consider first laying down slabs of 1-inch-thick rigid insulation. The joists rest directly on the insulation, but the "headers" on each edge of the platform rest directly on the existing floor. Which means they must be 1 inch higher, or shimmed to be 1 inch higher, than the cross beams.

Platform to create "sunken" look in living room can be 2-inch lumber framed over insulating panels. Plywood or particleboard can be adhered to frame with construction adhesive, as well as being nailed. Particleboard is less expensive than plywood, and does just as well for flooring.

To assure a rigid structure, spike short lengths of the 2-inch lumber between your platform joists to assure that the framing is rigid. Plywood or particleboard underlayment at least ⅝ inches thick is used for flooring. Where it's available, particleboard is strong enough, and much less expensive than plywood. Use hardened flooring nails to attach particleboard—it is quite dense—and do not nail closer than about ⅜ inch to the edges, as the material has a tendency to chip along the edges.

If the platform you build is not very high, you can add height to it with a psychological stunt that is sure to work. Use a railing up the steps, across the platform and down the steps. People are used to railings on stairways and subconsciously will consider the platform higher than it really is. And, the living room will appear "deeper" than

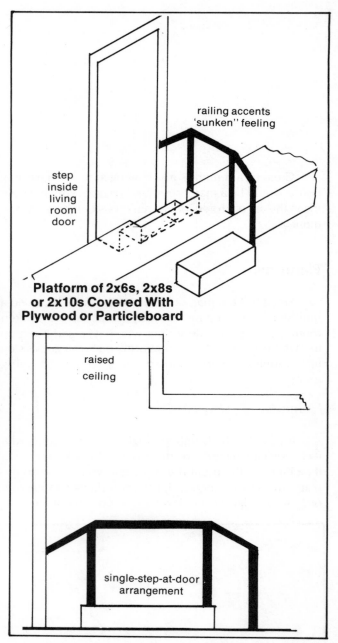

Platform of 2x6s, 2x8s or 2x10s Covered With Plywood or Particleboard

Railings up stairway, across platform and down the stairs creates strong psychological feeling that platform is higher than it really is, and living room is "deeper."

it really is. For an added effect, if you live in a one-story home, you can cut through the ceiling and frame a section a couple of feet higher than the rest so the platform has a raised ceiling over it. A light in the raised section will add to the feeling of height for both the platform and ceiling.

You can avoid the problems associated with the door, and the steps, by building the platform across the room from the door, or on one of the adjacent walls. As with the platform by the door, running carpeting up and over the platform will increase the "depth" of the rest of the room.

The platform, wherever it is located, will permit routing wiring, plumbing and even heat ducts where you want them. If you'd like a bar in your living room, but couldn't quite determine where the plumbing and drain could be located out of sight, the platform is an ideal solution.

The second-floor living room shown in the accompanying photo has a platform that provides a place for the furnace ducts, doubles as a seat and, in a pinch, can be used as a guest bed.

Storage

If storage is a problem in your remodeling, the platform can become a long cabinet by simply installing doors on the vertical face, rather than covering it with carpeting. Open shelves also could be used and, for really super storage, make the shelves on heavy plywood doors, so that pulling open a section of hinged shelving will expose a cabinet behind.

Paneling can be used to make steps appear higher by angling lines over stairs, as shown here. Note that carpeting is used on stair treads, but risers have wall paneling.

Platform entrance to this living room is built inside room, at right angles to the entrance door. Clever unifying touch uses floor tile on entrance wall. (Photo courtesy Azrock Floor Products)

Balconies and Dining Areas

If one end of your living room already is raised to create a "balcony" for the dining area, you can increase the "depth" of your sunken living room by installing a railing along the edge of the platform. The room will appear to be deeper by the height of the railing, or partial wall. The use of vertical-patterned wall paneling will make the height of the wall appear even greater.

Ceilings

Probably the simplest method of setting off part of the living room from the rest is to drop a section of the ceiling. That part of the room could be paneled, then a dropped ceiling, (as described in the first chapter on Basics) could be installed. Only part of the ceiling is dropped for this installation, then the paneling that is used on the walls is applied to the short wall down from the ceiling at the end of the dropped-ceiling area.

If paneling is not used, then plasterboard can be nailed to a framing of 2 x 2s or 2 x 4s. The paint or wallcovering used on the walls could also be applied to the "ceiling wall."

In this upstairs living room, platform at one end provides place for heat ducts, is seat and also an occasional guest bed. Low chair and cushion seat accentuate "depth" of this sunken living room. (Photo courtesy Wall Covering Information Bureau)

One of the several kinds of ceiling tile can be used to create soundproofing and quiet for dining, or for a conversation area or for a section over a bar. Such an area would be ideal for a music center.

Rather than having a chandelier hanging down, flush lights could be installed in the ceiling, with all the wiring hidden in that very useful area above the ceiling. Plumbing for a bar (plastic pipes and fittings) could also be run across inside the ceiling, then down to the bar inside a false wall behind or alongside the bar, or down through cabinets on the wall.

Raised Fireplaces

Another psychological means of accentuating different heights to make the living room feel "sunken" is to raise the fireplace several feet above the floor. See the chapter on fireplaces for free-standing units you can install yourself, almost anywhere in the living room. All that is necessary is a clear path up through the ceiling to the roof for the chimney.

Simulated masonry can be used for the platform under the fireplace; anyone sitting at floor level, looking up at the flames, will feel they are in a sunken area. If you have heavy, "blocky" modern furniture, you can arrange a "conversation pit" around the fireplace to accent the visual impression of a sunken area.

Even without a fireplace you can create a feeling of depth, and length, with the heavy type of furniture sometimes called "modular seating," or a similar name. Dropping the ceiling above the furniture and utilizing 2 x 4 framing and plasterboard will give an unusual appearance. Recess a large mirror in the wall—or set in a deep frame—to give the room a look of twice its real area.

Planning Ahead

Before you build any platforms or make any changes that require considerable construction work, sit down and carefully plan the job. Plan and plan again; measure and remeasure. Sit and look at that part of the room that will be changed or remodeled and try to picture how it will look after you make a major change.

How will the change relate to windows and doors in the room? Will it make the room look shorter or longer? Can the change be designed differently to avoid changing the dimensions of the room visually? If you have a Polaroid camera, make some photos of the wall, or that part of the room that will be changed.

Place a piece of translucent tracing paper over the picture and sketch on the paper your proposed changes.

Depth of sunken living room (walled-in, paneled, heated porch) is accented by railing on upper level. Wall also drops from ceiling, increasing height of wall. (Photo courtesy California Redwood Association)

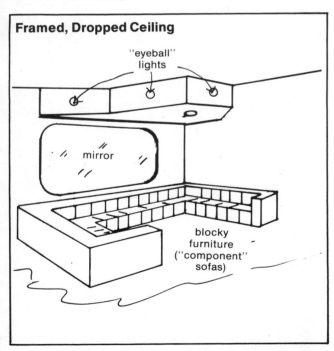

Framed, Dropped Ceiling

"eyeball" lights

mirror

blocky furniture ("component" sofas)

Heavy "modular" furniture, plus large mirror on the wall, aided by dropped ceiling that is framework covered with paneling or plasterboard, gives living room a unique appearance.

You can get a pretty fair idea of how the room will look after your changes, even if your skill at drawing is not too great.

The main idea is that now is the time to make changes—on paper, not after you've built something that will have to be torn apart and done over again. It might even be a good idea to make a scale model of your living room, say in a scale of 1 inch to the foot. Build and rebuild, change and rechange, but all in model size.

9. Cover Those Walls and Floors

The walls and floors in a room are the backdrop for your entire room arrangement. A ho-hum wall or floor is almost impossible to make exciting by adding accessories.

Walls

Redecorating walls can often be the simplest and most economical portion of a redecorating job. For instance an accent wall can be made to make a room appear longer, wider, or even higher. You can also change the shape and size of a room with color—inexpensive, easily applied coats of paint can work wonders. Not necessarily do you paint the whole room one color; one wall can be lighter than the others, and it will look closer. Paint it darker and it appears further away. With today's new painting materials, tools, and techniques a complete "color change" can be done quickly and easily.

If the room is narrow, horizontal patterns on the end wall will make that wall longer, and the room wider. Paneling or wall coverings can be used to do the trick. Run it horizontally instead of the usual vertical—unless you want the room to look higher.

If the wall surface is relatively flat and clean, paneling can be applied with panel adhesive from a caulking gun. A couple of ribbons on each one, press into place and you have a new wall.

Painting A "Problem Room"

A small room can be "expanded" if you paint it a light color. Be sure, too, to keep walls and woodwork the same color. Painting woodwork and trim in a different color from that of the wall will only create a cluttered look. A large room on the other hand, can be "cut down to size" by painting it in deeper colors with contrasting trim.

A room with a high ceiling is a common decorating problem. Bring a high ceiling down by painting it a deeper color than the walls. Square off a long, narrow, "bowl-ing alley" room by painting the two end walls in a warmer or deeper hue than the side walls.

If a perfectly square, uninteresting room needs a touch of excitement, paint one wall a bright, "eye-catching" color. And remember that any color in a large area looks "more so." Select a color sample that is lighter than the final results intended.

Purchasing Paint: Estimating Made Easy

Most walls and ceilings are rectangles. The formula for finding the area of a rectangle is Area = Length x Width. In this case, substitute the height of your wall for

Put a dramatic wallcover to work utilizing washable and strippable wallpaper. The more powerful the pattern, the better it masks the awkward transitions fairly common to many remodeling projects.

Often the simplest method of redoing walls is to recover them with wall coverings. This whimsical wall-covering design climbs the walls and the ceiling; white trim and accessories bring fashion to items from the local bargain basement.

111

This pattern, an updated version of the classic flamestitch design, gives this foyer instant chic even though furnishings are limited to a mirror, a bench, and one generous plant.

the "width" in the formula. Now just follow the formula: multiply the length of the wall by the height. This gives you the area of one wall. Do this for all four walls and add all the products together. This will give you the number of square feet to be covered. Don't bother to deduct for windows unless they total more than 100 square feet in size.

Here's an example: Suppose your walls are 8 feet high and each wall is 20 feet long. Simply multiply 20 x 8 (length times height) to get the area of one wall. The an-swer is 160 square feet. As 160 square feet is the area of each wall, and you have four walls, just add the four products together. 160+160+160+160=640. Your total wall area for the room is 640 square feet.

Now check the label on the paint can for a statement of how many square feet a gallon will cover. If this infor-mation is not given, ask your paint dealer.

To get the final answer, divide the number of sqaure feet to be painted by the number of square feet a gallon

For prepasted wallcoverings, dampen and place in position on wall—use a brush to edge out air bubbles.

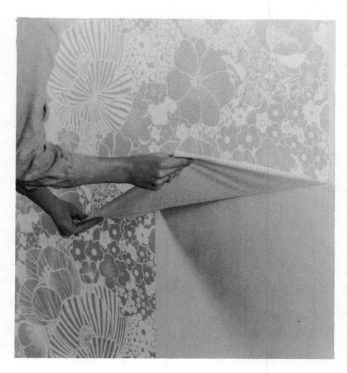

Strippable wallcoverings are easier to hang. You can lift up the wallcovering to correct a mistake, or even out a wrinkle, without fear of tearing the wallcovering.

A water tray right at the wall where you're working will save you many extra steps. These trays are available at wallcovering shops.

Make sure the edge is firmly applied before you go to the next strip.

Using today's sophisticated paints, materials, tools (like this paint pad), painting can be quick and easy and little mess.

1. Before installing, bring the material into the room where it will be placed, and stack it using full-length furring strips. This gives the panels time to adjust to the temperature and humidity in the room.

will cover. The result: the number of gallons or fractions of a gallon needed for the job. The same formula will work for estimating paint for any rectangular surface— like floors or ceilings.

Applying Paneling

Applying paneling to a room is quite simple compared to several years ago. All the tools you'll need are a saber saw, small square, ruler, caulking gun, some sort of long board as a straightedge, and hammer. If the walls are fairly straight and smooth you can often fasten paneling directly to the walls using either paneling brads or panel adhesive. However, in some cases, you may have to apply furring strips before you apply the paneling. These are simply 1 x 2's which can be purchased at the building supply dealer. They are nailed to the wall first, then the paneling nailed to them. Wooden shingles are used as shims behind the furring strips to bring them out equal and flush so the newly paneled wall won't have any dips or sags in it.

Space the furring 16 inches or 2 feet apart, on centers, so you can fasten the sheet edges to it properly.

Start the paneling on one end and make sure you get it true and perpendicular. If you don't, you'll end up with a see-saw effect at top and bottom of the panels as you go down the wall. Cut the top and bottom of the paneling to fit, measure for window openings, doors, etc. Remove the switch plate from receptacles, turn off electricity and pull out the receptacle a bit (leave it fastened to the wiring). Then measure for receptacle opening, use a template to cut around the opening and then place paneling over the receptacle, pull it through the opening and make sure receptacle will fit back in box properly. Fasten it in place if it

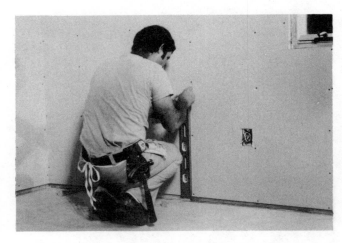

2. Walls need little preparation. On non-masonry wall, check it for a smooth, level, plumb surface, and mark stud locations on floor. You'll need wedges to hold panels ¼ inch off floor when you install them, and they should be ¼ inch from ceiling. Woodgrains will vary, so position all panels around room in best sequence, and mark them for position.

3. Begin paneling in a corner. Place panel there first and check for square, and mark off panel space with heavy marker. Mark imperfections that prevent panel from resting square, then trim panel to fit.

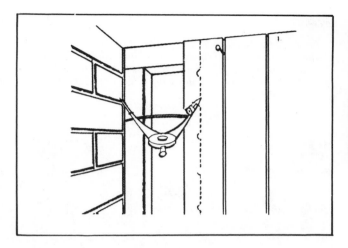

6. For outlet boxes, measure to edge of adjacent panel and mark area to be cut on the panel. Drill pilot holes in the corners of the space, then use a jigsaw or keyhole saw to cut area for outlet.

4. Plywood panels trim easily to fit into rough corners. If corner is very rough, scribe it with art compass (see drawing) and make panel conform by cutting, planing, filing or sanding.

7. Mitering moldings is simple, and finishes off the room. Work clockwise around the room for measurement, mark off the molding, then cut molding in a miter box.

5. You can nail panel all the way, but panel adhesive makes it easier. Apply beads of adhesive in 3-inch strips along edges, three waving beads between. Be generous with adhesive.

8. Before nailing moldings into place, compare angles for corners to check for accuracy, then nail molding into wall with brads.

Here are the steps for adding wainscot paneling using Marlite's package kit: (1) mark vertical line using plumb bob; (2) place panels using special edge clips to hold in position; (3) add a cap mold for trim along top edge. Below: completed installation.

does and then fasten paneling to wall using paneling brads, paneling adhesive or the new panel-clip units.

Paneling can be installed in the normal vertical installation in this manner, or even in a V shape if desired, to add an accent wall. Use prepainted matched plastic molding to trim out around wall top, bottom and corners.

There are a lot of paneling "substitutes" that can be used in place of paneling. Although they may simulate brick, stone, etc., they are installed in the same manner as paneling (see Chapter 3, "Accent Walls").

Floors

Refinishing Hardwood Floors

Rich, gleaming hardwood floors are an asset to any home. If your living room's hardwood floors have been dulled over the years, you can restore them to their former beauty. With the proper care, any do-it-yourselfer can refinish floors to an elegant sheen.

To begin with, remove the old finish. This is most efficiently done by sanding with an electric sander. Be careful not to let the moving sandpaper stay in one place too long; it can gouge a depression in the wood. Next, the floor should be examined for deep scratches. Wherever possible, sand the scratch out. If the scratch is too deep, it is sometimes possible to fill it with a plastic-sawdust compound. Allow the plastic material to dry thoroughly before sanding it smooth, flush to the floor.

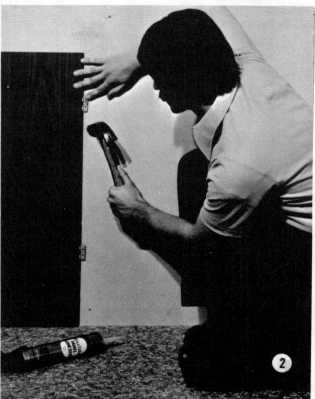

In addition to "paneling" there are many other styles of "rigid coverings" that simulate such things as brick and are installed in the same manner as paneling.

The final step before applying the finish is cleaning. A clean mop dampened with mineral spirits will be satisfactory for this job. Just take care not to wet the floor to any degree. Do not use an oil mop; oil will darken the wood and interfere later with the drying of the finish.

Some hardwoods, expecially oak, have pores which must be filled to create a smooth surface. If old filler is no longer intact, it is necessary to apply a new coat. Filler—either liquid or paste—is applied with a brush. First apply it across the grain, then apply it by brushing with the grain. Let the filler dry for a few minutes. Once the gloss has disappeared, remove the surplus. To do this you can work only on one area of the floor at a time. Wipe off the excess with burlap—first across the grain, then gently with the grain. Change to clean burlap frequently. The floor should be perfectly smooth if the filler has been applied correctly.

When the filler has dried completely (usually overnight), it's time to apply the sealer. Sealers are used as protective finishes for hardwood floors. They penetrate the fibers of the wood and form a wear-resistant surface which does not extend below the surface of the wood. Sealer is applied liberally, usually with long-handled lamb's wool or nylon applicators. First move across the grain of the wood, and then with the grain for complete coverage. If the manufacturer's directions indicate, wipe up the surplus with rags. After the proper drying time (see label), buff the surface with steel wool. An electric buffer makes this job fairly easy. Clean the floor thoroughly with a vacuum cleaner. Now apply a second coat. Make this coat thin and apply only with the grain.

After the sealer is dry, you may either wax the floor or apply varnish for added protection. Floor varnishes are available in several degrees of gloss. Selection of gloss is a matter of preference, but high gloss varnishes are usually more wear-resistant. If a sealer is not used, at least two varnish coats will be required to obtain a uniform appearance. Be sure to use a dust-free brush and work on a dust-free floor. Avoid excessive brushing—it may cause air bubbles. If air bubbles do appear, remove them by brushing back into the area with light feathering strokes before the varnish begins to set.

Machines are essential for floor refinishing, and can often be rented. A large drum-type sanding machine with vacuum attachment is best for main floor area, while a power edger does sides, as shown.

Hand scraping is sometimes needed at edges and in corners even with an edger-sander. Be careful with all sanding not to gouge, and go over the job enough times to create a good surface, sanding with the grain.

Floor Covering Materials

Carpeting and resilient flooring materials no longer are jobs strictly for the professional. Any handy home owner can lay carpeting, whether shag or sculptured or plush. The material is available in wide sections you can install with the aid of scissors and double-face tape. Alternately, you can install carpet squares, much like squares of vinyl floor tile. Both resilient tile and carpeting can be applied not only on the floor, but on the wall, for a very special look.

Resilient flooring—vinyl, vinyl asbestos, asphalt or rubber—can be installed either in sheets or in squares. Resilient floors clean easily.

Resilient carpeting materials—with a thin sponge backing that makes them comfortable to walk on—help insulate a room for both heat and noise. Carpeting is easily vacuumed and/or shampooed. Not only is resilient carpeting easily cleaned and long-lasting, you can purchase wall coverings with the identical color and pattern of the floor cover. This means you can apply panels of covering in frames of molding, even adhere it to cabinet doors.

Ceramic tile—an accent on floor or wall. Once the province of professionals only, ceramic tile now is definitely a do-it-yourself decorating material. Patterned ceramic tile also makes a beautiful hearth in front of, under, or around a fireplace (depending on the style of fireplace) and even on the walls adjacent to it. Entries to a living room become dramatic entrances when paved with ceramic tile. Like any ceramic material, it cleans easily, and wears well.

Self-Adhesive Tiles

For a quick economical floor covering try self-adhesive tiles. Most home owners consider the replacement of flooring a major expense and problem; indeed, at one time it was. Not only did you have to pay to have the old flooring torn up, but there was substantial extra labor involved in smoothing out the subfloor, spreading adhesives, and cutting and fitting the new material.

Today the job is easy—thanks to the new self-adhering floor tiles that come with their own adhesive, pre-applied to the back. In many cases, these tiles can be laid directly over your present floor. Doing the work yourself, it's possible to cover an average 10-foot-by-15-foot area in less than four hours. And because you do the work yourself, you save the cost of a professional installer.

Self-adhering tiles are made of the same sturdy vinyl-asbestos formulation that's been a favorite of do-it-yourselfers for years. The key difference between these and conventional floor tiles is that there's no messy adhe-

sive to spread. You simply peel off a protective paper backing, place the tile over your old floor, and press.

Any resilient floor can be covered in this manner, provided the old material is smooth and well bonded to the subfloor. All that's necessary in the way of preparation is to clean the surface, making sure that all old wax is removed. Then simply measure out the job according to instructions in the tile package, and begin laying your new floor.

Self adhering tiles are available in a wide range of attractive styles and colors. Other than a few common household tools, the tile is all you need to create a beautiful new surface underfoot.

Sheet Flooring

Perhaps you prefer the look of the no-wax sheet flooring.

No-wax floors require so little maintenance—all that's necessary is sweeping or vacuuming and an occasional sponge-mopping with detergent, followed by a thorough rinse—that they're popping up wherever the homemaker wants convenience and style.

So it's no surprise to find a no-wax floor in a room other than the kitchen and bath where standard resilient floors have long held sway.

Some people prefer the easy care and good looks of a no-wax floor and the coziness of carpet at the same time.

Steps in laying floor tiles are just about the same whether all-vinyl or vinyl-asbestos tiles are being used. Cutting of all-vinyl tiles is easy with a scissors while the vinyl asbestos type tiles may better be cut with scoring tools or a tile cutter. Layout of starting center lines is important to get good tile alignment and photo (1) indicates careful measurement to obtain proper perpendicular center lines. In (2), tile units are temporarily laid out to check border widths and thus verify suitable position for center lines. Once the lines are established and marked on the underlayment, adhesive is spread (3) with a brush or notched adhesive trowel keeping within one quarter of the room. A short wait may be needed (4) until the surface of the adhesive feels tacky to the touch rather than wet.

Tile units are started at the juncture of the center lines and work of laying unit by unit proceeds toward the outer edges (5). When all field tile have been laid carefully butting each new tile to the adjoining tiles, it's time to work on the border tiles. First, in (6), the full tile piece to be cut for border installation is held on top of last full tile for marking. A line drawn across edge marks allows accurate cutting (7) and then in (8), the cut border piece is slipped into place first butting it to the last previous tile. For many resilient floor covering installations, vinyl cove base is an appropriate trim that lends a hand in floor maintenance by keeping floor corners clean. In (9), cove base is being applied and in (10), the final step: rolling the tiles in both directions using a heavy steel floor roller.

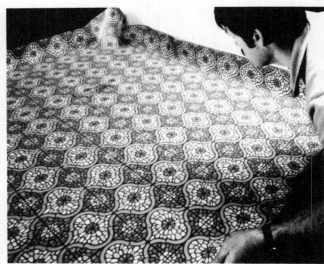

Sheet Vinyl Installation Procedure for Armstrong's Tredway line of cushioned vinyl coverings but the steps are applicable for other, similar products. The covering is intended for application by stapling of edges and use of adhesive where the staple gun can't reach or where there is no show mold to hide the staples. Adhesive can be used for installation over concrete floors, too. The steps begin (1) with roll up of material face out. Rolls come in 12 foot and 6 foot widths; the wide material can be installed without a seam in some rooms while a single seam near the room center wioll be suitable for larger rooms. In (2), the first piece of floor covering is unrolled and excess allowed to extend up walls or offsets such as cabinets; couble-sided carpet tape is stretched along both sides of the center seam, paper covering off on the floor side but remaining in place on the covering side. Next in (4), the second vinyl sheet is unrolled and its edge is brought to just overlap the first sheet.

Photo (6) is a close-up of the overlap indicating that the sheets have been adjusted for pattern match. A utility knife is used to cut out a U-shaped section from the excess extending up the wall or cabinet at both seam ends so that the seam area will lie flat on the underlayment. And then in (7), the knife with the help of a steel straightedge is used to cut through both vinyl sheets to produce a perfectly butted seam. Photo (8) indicates lifting of sheet edges to pull out top paper covering from the carpet tape and pull away the trimmed off portion of the under vinyl sheet. In (9), seam sealing cement or adhesive is being applied.

The installation is completed by trimming at borders and fitting around cabinet corners. Shown here in (10) is an upward knife cut of the floor covering at an inside corner in order to permit covering to be fitted tightly down. In photo (11), an outside cabinet corner is to be trimmed and the corner cut is started at the floor line. A steel straightedge (12) is used for cutting along wall or cabinet and the floor covering sheet is turned back (13) to allow application of adhesive or cement. Finally a manual staple gun is used with ⅜ to ⁹⁄₁₆ inch long staples spaced at about 3-inch intervals. Edge and staples are then covered with a base show molding strip.

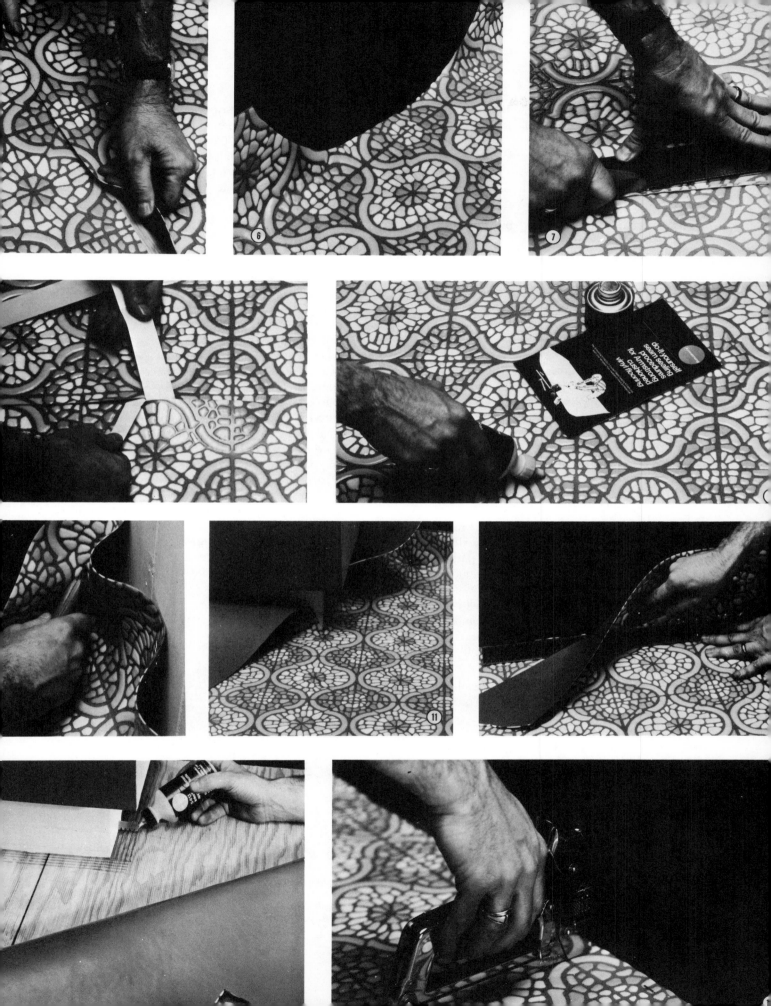

This explains the growing popularity of wall-to-wall expanses of no-wax flooring dotted with plain or fancy area rugs.

Each season brings new pattern in the latest styles and colors to vie for her attention. Today new types of cushioned vinyl floors are quick and easy to install because:

(1) they can be fastened down by stapling around the edges of a room;

(2) they are flexible, not at all "boardy" or semi-rigid like other vinyl floors, and can actually be folded like a blanket; (sheet flooring comes in continuous rolls, as opposed to individual tiles.)

(3) they have a built-in margin for error. The do-it-yourselfer can trim them less than perfectly but still obtain a perfect fit; the material with stretch!

Installation—the recommended installation calls for stapling the floor around the edges of the room to fasten it down. Cement is applied at the edges in places a staple gun can't reach, such as under an overhang, or where there is no baseboard or molding to hide staples. Cement is also used for installations over subfloors, like concrete, that staples won't penetrate.

Carpeting

Wall-to-wall carpet is today the single most popular furnishing in U.S. homes. Not only does carpet beautify...it unifies other furnishings, particularly in cut-up rooms disrupted by hectic architecture, built-ins, fireplaces, and too many doors or windows. Owners of older homes are using wall-to-wall carpet not only because it looks luxurious, but because it completely hides neglected or worn-out floors that can't be repaired. Carpet also eliminates most surface noises, like footsteps, moving furniture, etc.

If you've been putting off installing wall-to-wall carpet because of the expense, you can stop procrastinating now.

It's quite possible to do the job yourself with self-stick carpet squares, and the cost is economically feasible. For one thing, you don't have to buy additional padding since cushioning is already built in.

Carpet squares are versatile. They come in myriad styles and colors. There are sculptured shag, level-loop—styles to fit any decor. Carpet squares are also "forgiving"—mistakes can be disguised or rectified easily. And they are portable. Packaged ten squares to a box, you can predetermine the approximate cost per square foot, estimate the number of packs and/or cartons needed, and drive away from the store with the potential wall-to-wall carpet in the trunk of your car.

You'll not only increase comfort...but add color and beauty to your home when you use carpet squares. Nothing can give a room a "lift" like wall-to-wall carpet!

Here's how simple it is to install squares:

(1) Measure the room to find its center point. Use a carpenter's square to make sure you have a 90° angle.

(2) Peel back the protective paper from each square as you work and lay a row of loose squares along the chalk lines in one quarter of the room in the shape of a large "L".

(3) To fit the squares along the room perimeter, place a loose square on top of the last full square, pile side down. Then take a second square and fit it against the wall. Make a pencil line on the paper back of the first square; cut the piece and drop it into place.

(4) In or around an irregular area like a pipe, simply make a paper pattern of the space you must fill or allow for; trace the pattern on the square and shape it with scissors or knife.

For a finishing touch on exposed edges in doorways, use metal door trim or reducer strips available at dealer or hardware stores. While not absolutely necessary, shoe molding nailed to the baseboard over carpet edges will give a trim, professionally installed look to a finished floor.

More people every year are saving money on residential carpet by doing the installation work themselves, and they are only the "average type" handy persons. A few hours investment produces results that literally transform a room with no mess or fuss.

You can also install wall-to-wall carpet with no fuss ... no muss using carpet squares. Locate the center point of the room, and simply peel the protective paper from the carpet square, press firmly in place, and cover the room.

Install Your Own Shag Carpet

Few areas of home decorating produce more dramatic results than the installation of wall-to-wall carpet. Whether used to cover an old unsightly floor, or simply for decorative interest, new carpet always seems to create instant warmth and coziness...not to mention the excitement it can add to an interior color scheme.

As an alternative to carpet tiles, shag carpet in roll form is easy to install. In fact, once the job is done, you'll be hard pressed to distinguish it from a professional installation.

"Do-it-yourself" carpet comes in 12-foot wide rolls and incorporates a high density foam backing which eliminates the need for separate padding. Roll edges are precision-cut at the factory and simply butt together. This means there is no complicated cutting or fitting at the seams.

Installation is easy. Simply roll the carpet out on the floor and trim with a pair of heavy shears to fit along room edges. Apply double-faced carpet tape at the seams to hold adjacent pieces snugly together.

Installation Of Roll Carpeting

To install do-it-yourself shag carpet, first run a piece of heavy chalk around the perimeter of the room, leaving marks on both the baseboard (or wall surface) and the floor.

Precut factory edges guarantee straight seams with continuation. The carpet needs to be taped down only at seams and doorways with double-faced tape for a secure bond.

Roll carpet out on the floor, allowing excess to run up the wall a few inches, and firmly press carpet into the floor-wall joint. This will cause the chalklines to be transferred to the carpet backing as shown. Then simply cut with heavy shears between the two lines for a perfect room edge fit.

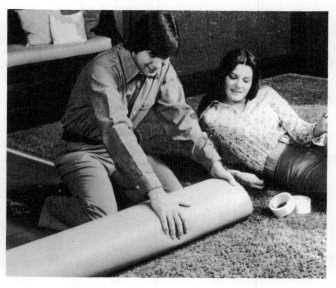

Second roll is fitted into place alongside the first and held securely by tape. The shag texture does an effective job of concealing seams and produces a rich finished appearance.

Carpets near a fireplace should be noncombustible, like this hearth rug called the "Blaze-ban", made of Fiberglas.

10. Fireplaces

A fireplace is usually the focal point of any room. If you have an existing fireplace, there are many ways you can change the exterior of the fireplace to make it fit your decor. You can add a mantle, remove one, or add more molding to a wooden faced fireplace. You can put down new ceramic tile on the hearth, strip off old paint, or paint on new paint. You can make a mantle smaller or larger, etc. You cannot however, change the inside firebox dimensions of the fireplace without some trouble. One the other hand, if you don't have a fireplace but are considering one, there are many decisions to be made: style, facing material; whether or not it will have a heat circulator; whether it will be for looks only, or will be a functional heating unit for the room or area; front opening; side see-through, and so on. Although a fireplace installation can be a do-it-yourself project utilizing one of the metal forms (such as those sold by Superior or Heatilator), it's still a pretty fair project involving many hours of work, some specialized tools, and a fair knowledge of carpentry and masonry. This is not to say that an average do-it-yourselfer can't do the job, but it's wise to talk to someone that has tackled the job before cutting a hole in the wall. Entire books have been written illustrating how a step-by-step project such as this is done.

Rejuvenating An Old Fireplace

You can revitalize an old fireplace which has been coated with many years of paint by stripping off the old paint. Since it's almost impossible to get all the paint out of the crevices, the result gives the look of "used brick" which is so popular and expensive today.

The first step is to remove any furniture from the area and cover walls and floor with at least two layers of newspapers. We found the stripping very effective but quite sloppy, so you may have to repaint walls after the job is done. Use only a good quality paste-type stripper, the thin liquid kinds just won't stay on the vertical surfaces long enough to work properly. Brush the stripper on in a full

Built-in bookshelves offer an excellent way to utilize the space on either side of a fireplace.

The Anatomy of a Fireplace

Chimney Cap

Available precast for some standard flue sizes or cast in place. Note that the liner projects through the cap several inches.

Smoke Chamber

Together with the smoke shelf, this area is important to a smoke free fire. Both sides slope to the flue and it is important that they slope identically, otherwise the fire will burn on one side of the firebox only.

The entire smoke chamber and smoke shelf is parged with fire clay mortar (refractory mortar) or type "S" mortar one-half inch thick.

Throat and Damper

These parts are usually one and the same. The damper is capable of being opened and closed gradually to control the draft and keep out cold air when the fireplace is not in use. The opening in square inches should be at least 90% of that required for the flue.

Firebox

This is the area that comes alive with dancing flames and gleaming embers. To do this the firebox must be correctly proportioned, sealed, vented, and well constructed.

Hearth

The inner hearth is that portion within the fire area and is usually built of fire brick but may be other types of hard brick, concrete, stone, tile or other non-combustible heat-resistant materials. The outer hearth is built of the same type materials and should extend a minimum of eight inches on each side of the fireplace opening and sixteen inches in front. (Note: These figures are twelve inches and eighteen inches in areas covered by the Uniform Building Code.)

Flue and Flue Lining

The area of the flue should equal one-twelfth to one-eighth the area of the opening of the fireplace (width times height). Lining is supported on masonry.

Smoke Shelf

This is a horizontal shelf, usually concave and extending backward from the rear of the throat or damper to the rear flue wall. It directs cold air downdrafts which are present in the early stages of the fire, causing them to eddy and drift upward with the rising air currents.

Ashpit

This is the hollow space below the hearth into which ashes fall through the ash dump door located in the hearth. A metal door is provided in the ashpit for the occasional removal of ashes. In basementless homes, particularly those buit on a concrete slab, it may not be feasible to provide an ashpit unless the hearth has been raised. In this case the ashpit door faces outside.

Foundation

Consult your local building code, since these codes differ according to existing soil and moisture conditions in individual areas. If total weight is needed to compute the depth and rise of the foundation required, figure brick at 130 lbs. and concrete at 150 lbs. per cubic foot. For cubic footage, figure the entire cross section volume including the open portion of the flue and firebox. The footing should extend at least below the depth of the greatest frost penetration.

As a general rule, footings should be of concrete at least twelve inches thick and should extend at least six inches on all sides of the foundation. Concrete should be poured on undisturbed soil.

Foundation walls should be a minimum of eight inches thick.

CHIMNEY CAP

FLUE LINER

MANTLE

FLUE

SMOKE CHAMBER

SMOKE SHELF

LINTEL

DAMPER

FIRE BOX

ASH DUMP

HEARTH

ASH PIT DOOR

ASH PIT

coat starting at the top of the fireplace. Allow it to work, giving it plenty of time. If the top coat of paint isn't loosening and bubbling up all over, paint on more stripper. Don't attempt to remove the stripper until all the top coat has loosened, and don't allow the stripper to dry on the surface. When the surface has loosened, remove as much as possible with a wide scraper, putting the stripper and removed paint in an old can.

Wear rubber gloves during the entire operation. Cover your eyes with goggles or face shield and wear old clothes.

When the bulk of material has been removed, use a coarse steel bristle brush dipping it in cold water to scrub away the rest of the material. Steel wool dipped in clean water can be used for the final clean-up of the fireplace. Then scrape away debris from the hearth and treat it in the same manner to remove the old paint. Scrub down again with clear water and a brush to remove any tiny bits of paint that still may be adherring to the fireplace.

Painting

On the other hand a fireplace can often be made less noticeable in a room by painting it a color the same as the walls of the room. However, after stripping the paint from an otherwise beautiful fireplace, you will realize that paint can provide some real future problems. If you do decide to paint, use a washable paint in one of the epoxies.

Fireplace Face-Lift

Our old country home has one of the best fireplaces in the world. You can light a match anywhere in the living room and watch the smoke head for the chimney. The fireplace was constructed about 60 years ago for heat, and that it does. During a recent midwinter power black-out, we had to do without a furnace, and the fireplace going full blast day and night more than heated the house. Our only complaint was the appearance. Old, dingy, and out of date; the fireplace didn't quite fit our idea of a cozy country farmhouse. Yet, we didn't wish to sacrifice the possibility of losing it's functionality by completely redoing it. Our solution was to give it a minor facelift, which did not affect the operation of the fireplace, but quite transformed our living room.

The first step was to make the hearth larger. In the days when the fireplace was built, the surrounding wooden floor didn't need a lot of protection from sparks.

An old fireplace was given a new look by cleaning bricks and applying new paneling.

A fireplace doesn't have to be flat against the wall, there are several free-standing or corner fireplaces such as the one shown.

Before: An old painted fireplace can often be stripped of the old paint.

After: Result is the popular "used-brick" look.

Rejuvenating The "Old Painted" Fireplace

Allow stripper to work old paint loose then scrub off of brick and out of crevices using a steel bristle brush. Wear rubber gloves, eye or face protectors and old clothes.

First step is to cover walls and floors with at least two layers of newspaper. Then brush on a full coat of stripper, starting at the top.

Do hearth in same manner, then flush with plenty of clean water and mop up loosened paint, water, etc.

Before: Old fireplace is out of style, appears top heavy.

After: After rejuvenating, old fireplace takes on new appearance and fits room better.

We lived in the house for three years before we decided to install carpeting, so we merely measured the burn marks on the floor and made our hearth to fit. Now with the enlarged hearth, we have little danger of sparks settling into the carpet. Because the hearth set up about ¼ inch above the wooden floor, enlarging it first meant laying a subfloor around the original concrete hearth, so the hearth tile would lay flat. Pieces of ¼ inch plywood were nailed in position, making sure the hearth was square on all sides. Then the nails were "dimpled," or set slightly under the wood surface with a hammer and the nail heads and all cracks filled with water putty. The joining crack between the cement and wood subfloor was sealed using latex patching cement. Then a coarse belt on a belt sander was used to smooth down the entire hearth area, leaving a smooth level surface for installing the ceramic tile.

Incidentally, if you install ceramic tile on any surface, it must be absolutely smooth and flat or the tiles will rock and not only adhere poorly, but may break or crack from the pressure of walking them.

With the hearth area smooth and flat, it was vacuumed to remove all dust and debris, then a ceramic tile adhesive spread over the surface using a toothed mastic spreader. The sheets of ceramic tile were carefully fitted in place, then pushed down solidly so they would set in the mastic properly. This was allowed to set overnight, then latex tile grout in a natural mortar color to match the color of the tiles was mixed and spread over the tiles, forcing it down in the cracks between the tiles with a putty knife. After ensuring that all cracks were thoroughly filled, the excess grout was removed using a wet sponge, followed by a damp cloth. Because the latex grout sets so fast, you can do only a small area at a time, or it may set up to the point it becomes hard to work. On a small area such as the hearth, this was no problem. After washing with a damp cloth, go over the entire tile surface with a dry, clean cloth to polish the tiles and remove any remaining grout dust. You may wish to do this again after allowing the grout to set for a couple of hours.

The first step has been completed; the next step was to build a mantel to fit over the fireplace. The mantel shown is merely a wooden box made of rough-sawn cedar 1 x 12's; it fits over the mantel and up against the front and sides. The main thing is to make sure the mantel is tightly fitted to the fireplace so there are no open holes in which mice can crawl. When we removed the old mantel, the hollow space in it was literally filled with mice nests. Incidentally, this is also a great place to install a secret hiding place for valuables.

After fitting the mantel to the fireplace, it was removed, stained and finished, then reinstalled and screwed permanently in place to the surrounding wall studs and window trim. Make sure the mantel is level in all directions and follows the lines of the bricks on the fireplace. It would look silly if the mantel set cock-eyed on the fireplace, even though it might rest perfectly flat on the top bricks.

The last step in rejuvenating was to install artificial

First step was to nail down subfloor or ¼-inch plywood to extend hearth out into room.

After nailing down subfloor, water putty was mixed and cracks filled in. Nail heads were "dimpled," or set.

Then new hearth area was sanded smooth with belt sander and coarse grit belt.

Expand The Hearth Area...

Mastic was applied to hearth area . . .

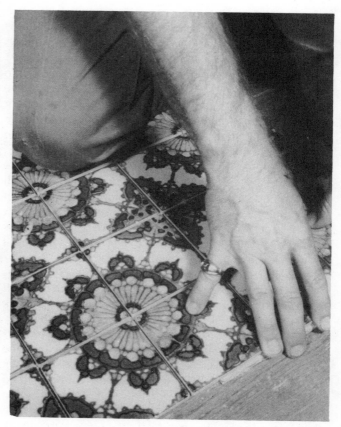

And decorative ceramic tile placed on mastic. Tile shown comes in sheets, is easy and quick to install, if you make sure you follow the pattern.

Add A Mantel

A mantel is assembled and fitted in place, then stained and fastened in place permanently.

After tile has set overnight, grout is mixed using matching-color, latex grout and special grout mixing liquid. Grout is forced down in cracks using spatula or putty knife.

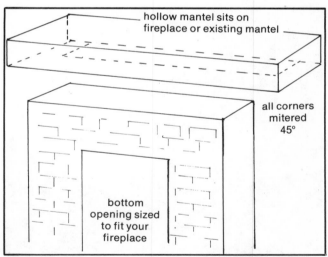

Mantel is a wooden box made from 1x12-inch rough sawn cedar. Be sure the mantel fits tightly to the wall.

Then a damp sponge or cloth is used to remove excess grout and to clean tile.

131

brick panels on each side of the old fireplace to extend the appearance of the fireplace out to the two windows on each side. The bricks shown are fiberglass and look so much like real brick, it's hard to tell where the fireplace stops and the artificial bricks begin.

The first step for installation of the "brick panels" is to cut them to fit between the fireplace and the window trim. The back side of the brick panels is then coated with panel adhesive and the bricks installed in place. You may have to drive small flat-headed nails in between the bricks in the panels to help hold the panels in place until the panel adhesive sets up. After all brick panels are installed, a realistic sand-filled grout which resembles brick mortar is squeezed between the bricks, then worked with your fingers until it fits the surrounding brick-mortar pattern.

The final step is to install the fireplace screen, tools, and hang your favorite art object above your "new" fireplace.

Back ribbings of artificial brick are coated with mastic . . .

And brick panels placed in position.

Decorative fiberglass brick panels were used to finish outsides of fireplace between actual bricks and window casing. First step is to cut to proper size using hack saw.

Special grout that appears like real brick-mortar is applied between bricks to give appearance of real brick wall.

You can also add an elegant and functional fireplace to any room with Z-Brick, particleboard framing and a prefabricated metal firebox.

Building A Working Fireplace Without Masonry

It used to be that if you wanted to add a brick or stone fireplace to your home, you had to have brick or stone...plus all the weight, mess and expense of having these cumbersome materials installed.

Now, ready-installed metal fireboxes and chimneys allow you to build a working fireplace in almost any room without using conventional masonry. In a typical installation, wood framing is then covered with plywood or particle board, which serves as a base for decorative covering.

The rugged, warm appearance of brick and stone is also possible with these "prefabricated" fireplaces. All you need is nonceramic decorative brick or fieldstone. Make sure the product you choose is fireproof.

Given here are steps for finishing off a working fireplace with Z-BRICK. First you must select the proper size firebox. These fireboxes are available from several manufacturers in widths from 28 inches up to 42 inches, with both right and left open-end, or open-front, configura-

tions. Most units may be placed directly on a combustible floor, against a combustible wall, or raised on a wooden platform. The only areas where clearances are required are near the flue, portions of the hearth, and the entire from opening surface.

Framing for the fireplace and hearth may be constructed entirely from 2 x 4's and 2 x 2's. To complete the carpentry work, the firebox is set in place, framed, and the plywood or particle board walls installed. Of course, framing for the flue must also be finished before the particle board walls are erected.

With framing completed, and the firebox, flue and chimney assemblies in place (instructions for flue and chimney are included in the manufacturer's installation instructions), you can begin application of the brick.

Enough Z-BRICK or stone should be on hand based on a coverage of 5 to 6 square feet per carton. You'll need 1 gallon of adhesive mortar for every 16 square feet of brick surfaces, and 1 quart of sealer for every square feet of "bricked" area.

Tools required are a hacksaw for cutting (no special tile or brick cutter is necessary), broad-bladed putty knife,

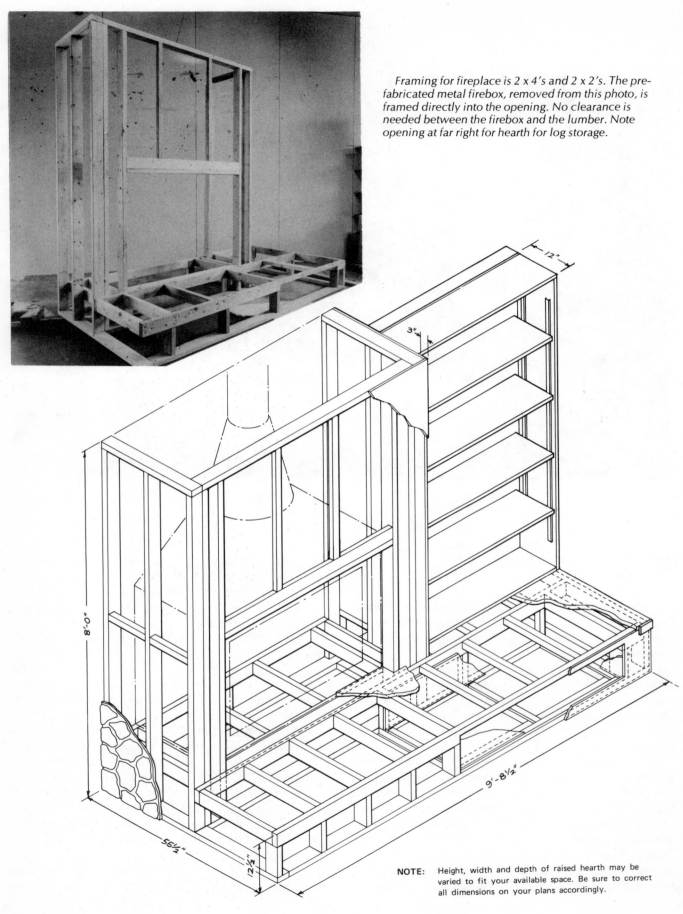

Framing for fireplace is 2 x 4's and 2 x 2's. The pre-fabricated metal firebox, removed from this photo, is framed directly into the opening. No clearance is needed between the firebox and the lumber. Note opening at far right for hearth for log storage.

12"

3"

8'-0"

9'-8½"

55½"

12½"

NOTE: Height, width and depth of raised hearth may be varied to fit your available space. Be sure to correct all dimensions on your plans accordingly.

coarse rasp, small stiff brush, and paper towels or clean rags.

The rasp is used to shape bricks and for mitering corners. It should also be used to remove irregularities from the bricks and stones as they come out of the cartons.

To apply Z-BRICK, start by spreading adhesive mortar on about a 4-square-foot area of the surface to be covered. Use the broad-bladed knife to spread to a thickness of about $1/16$th inch. Next, press the brick or stone into place with a wiggling or sliding motion. Mortar should squeeze up into the space between the bricks.

A mortar line of about ⅜ inch should be observed for Z-BRICK...but not too perfectly to give a more authentic look. With stone, irregular spaces from ½" to ¾" should be left between pieces. Mortar between the joints should be smoothed with a small stick or brush. And any mortar on the surface of the brick or stone should be cleaned up immediately with a damp towel or cloth.

After the brick has been laid, the mortar should be left to harden for about three days. Then, one or two coats of sealer should be brushed on to protect and seal the surface.

Several plan sheets are available for fireplaces using prefabricated metal fireboxes and Z-Brick. The plans include designs for a large fireplace with a log storage area in the hearth and a build-in bookcase (Order: Woodbin Hearth Fireplace Plans, see Appendix), a smaller unit with

log storage plus several rustic mantle designs, (Order: Country Rustic Fireplace Plans), a compact fireplace framed by a graceful brick arch (order: Arch Fireplace Plans), a complete floor-to-ceiling model with storage cabinets (Order: Room Divider Fireplace Plans), a simple "flat wall" fireplace with early American design and wooden mantle (Order: Traditional Fireplace Plans), and finally, a difficult, but elegant pyramid design ideal for cabins or ski lodges (Order: Pyramid Fireplace Plans). Be sure to specify the title of the plans you wish to order. Plans are available by writing to Z-BRICK, Woodinville, Wa. 98072.

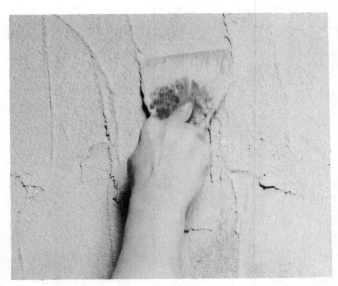

First step in applying Z-Brick is spreading the adhesive mortar on the particleboard. It is applied with a broad-bladed putty knife to a thickness of about $1/16$th inch. About a 4 foot square section should be prepared at one time.

Plywood or particleboard is installed over the framing before applying Z-Brick. Note firebox has been removed for photo.

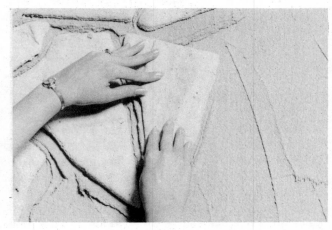

Brick or field stone pieces are pressed into place with a wiggling or sliding motion. Note that the mortar is pushed up into the spaces between the pieces of stone.

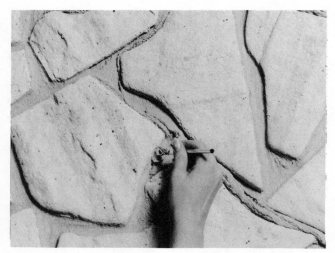

The excess mortar between stones is smoothed with a small brush or stick. Two of the brushes and a 3 inch knife are provided in a Z-Brick installation kit.

After brick has set 24 hours a couple of coats of sealer are applied.

Free-Standing Fireplaces

Another alternative to the traditional stone or brick fireplace is to utilize one of the new free-standing units. These can be installed in almost any location and are sold through most building supply houses and larger mail-order businesses. They can be installed by almost anyone utilizing ordinary carpenter tools. They utilize a metal asbestos lined flue that can be installed through the roof. The "fireplace" sets on a fireproof flooring installed first. If the fireplace is near a wall, the area near the fireplace must also be covered with a noncombustible material.

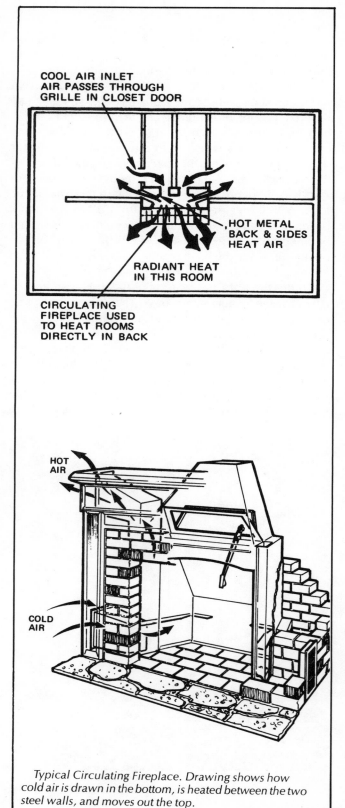

COOL AIR INLET
AIR PASSES THROUGH
GRILLE IN CLOSET DOOR

HOT METAL
BACK & SIDES
HEAT AIR

RADIANT HEAT
IN THIS ROOM

CIRCULATING
FIREPLACE USED
TO HEAT ROOMS
DIRECTLY IN BACK

HOT AIR

COLD AIR

Typical Circulating Fireplace. Drawing shows how cold air is drawn in the bottom, is heated between the two steel walls, and moves out the top.

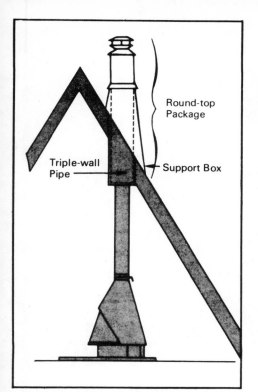

A-frame roofs pose no installation problems with the proper chimney package.

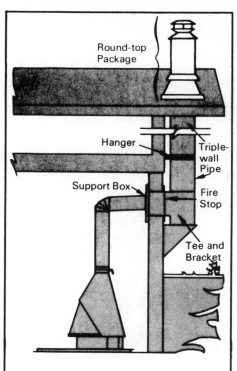

No need to cut through the attic. It's easy to elbow through an outside wall and vent straight up, using Tee and Bracket.

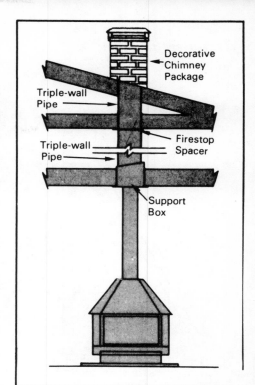

First floor installation in a two-story house. Chimney can be concealed in a second story closet.

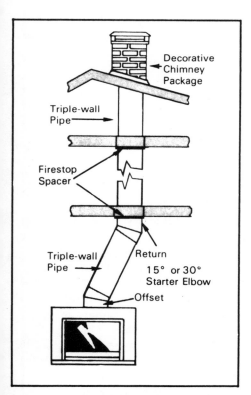

Preway chimneys clear upstairs obstructions with 15° or 30° elbows (all elbow kits include offset and return).

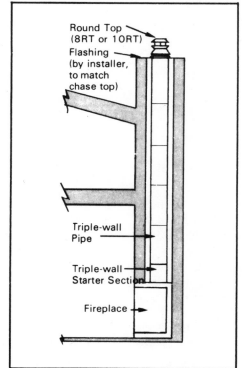

Today's space saving chase installations are a natural with Preway built-in fireplaces and chimney system.

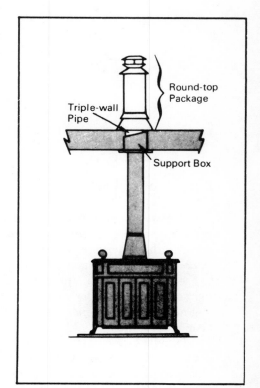

Installation through a flat roof is simple and the most economical of all.

Both fireplaces and wood burning stoves can be installed in a variety of ways: The six illustrations here detail some typical methods of chimney installation (photo courtesy of Preway).

137

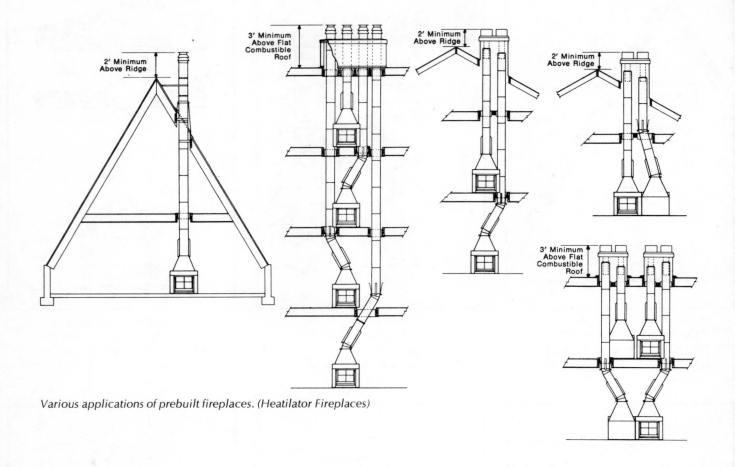

Various applications of prebuilt fireplaces. (Heatilator Fireplaces)

Fireplace Designs

At one time every living room had a fireplace, and in those days it was purely functional. Although many homes today have fireplaces in them, unless they are designed properly, maintained, and correctly, they can be worse than useless. A fireplace not equipped or designed right or operated properly can actually waste heated air that has cost a lot in energy from a furnace or electrical heating system.

Fireplace design is now just catching up with the rest of the building industry, and the past few years has seen a great deal of thinking going into how to make fireplaces more effective. The old-fashioned type of fireplace was effective to some degree but in relation to the amount of energy burned, the amount that actually heats the room is nominal. In addition a fireplace can be a real energy waster when not in use.

Saving Energy

There are, however, several things you can do not only when building a new fireplace, but to an old one as well. The first step is to insure that the fireplace is kept clean. Before season starts drop an old sack filled with old tire chains or similar materials down the fireplace to clean out any birds nests, knock away tar and pitch that collects from soft woods, and in general keep flue liner clean. Then check the damper and make sure it is working properly. If damper is not working properly have someone fix it, or, if you don't have a damper, which happens not infrequently on older fireplaces, have one installed by a competent fireplace construction contractor. One of the best energy savers you can install on a fireplace is a glass door. These not only can prevent sparks from setting your rug on fire, they can save a great deal of energy when the fireplace is not in use.

A typical home-owner installation utilizing a fireplace form and bricks.

A Choice
Of Designs

Fireplace designs have changed a great deal in the past few years for more energy efficient uses. This unit features a stainless steel heat exchanger.

This particular unit vents heated air to furnace for a better combination of the two.

Fireplaces can also be free-standing units which require only protection around them and a special flue.

An advanced design grate can also make an old fireplace much more efficient. Heated air is expelled from the hollow tubes of the grate.

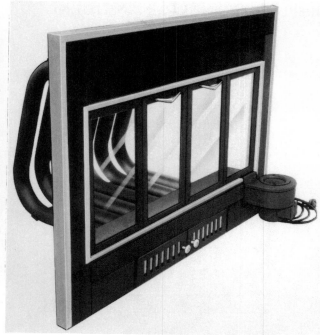

An even more advanced design utilizes the heated pipes plus a glass front and small blower on front to force heat into room.

A convection heating grate can also be a great help, and when combined with a glass fireplace screen and blower unit to bring heated air into the room, it can be a tremendous help. One excellent example of such a unit is the Thermograte Model Company.

A different approach is in Bill Hiser's new fireplace unit which ties to the central heating ducts. Bill's fireplace uses any solid fuel—wood, coal, even tightly rolled newspapers—to supply heat to the entire building in which it is installed. A simple interconnection with the central thermostat assures that whenever the fireplace is lit it is called on first to supply required heat anywhere in the building. The main furnace operates only when the fireplace is not lit or when it is unable to supply all the heat required. Thus the homeowner can use as much or as little solid fuel as he wants, whenever he wants to supplement or even replace his dependence on increasingly scarce and ever more costly natural gas.

And, unlike most fireplaces, this fireplace uses the solid fuel very efficiently. Most fireplaces are extremely inefficient for two reasons:

(1) only radiant heat directly from the fire is used.— The rest of the heat produced in fact almost all of it, goes straight up the chimney;
(2) even worse, preheated house air is used to support combustion and goes up the chimney with the smoke—with a conventional fireplace it is

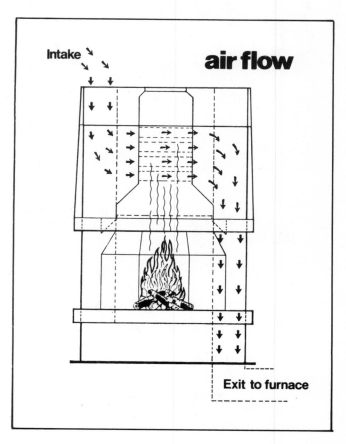

Intake

air flow

Exit to furnace

FIREPLACE FACINGS USING MOLDING

Mouldings above fireplace repeat basic mantel design.

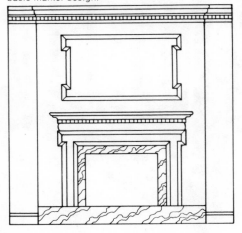

Mouldings used to coordinate fireplace and wall design.

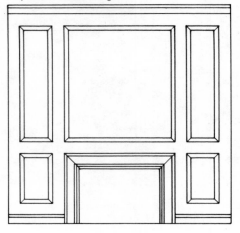

Mantel created with crown moulding and S4S stock.

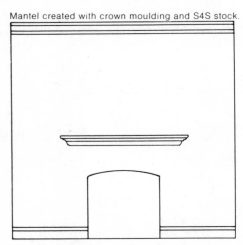

Simple mantel using S4S and crown.

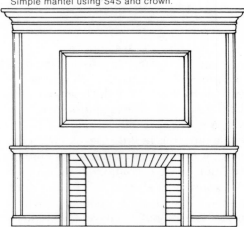

A contemporary fireplace accented by applying moulding in vertical rows.

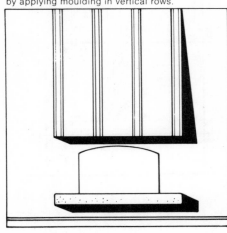

Mantel of S4S and crown coordinates beautifully with applied mouldings and paneling.

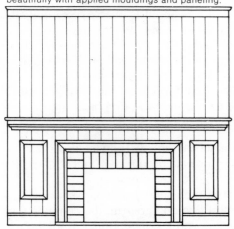

Or utilize a stove such as this Franklin Fireplace heater to do double duty of heating as well as cooking foods. (Photo courtesy of United States Stove Co.)

Clean lines and efficient heat are main attractions of this stove by Majestic.

not unusual for the fireplace to remove more heated air from the home than it gives back, which means that the central furnace actually has to work harder when the fireplace is lit.

The Lighthouse fireplace solves both of these problems in a single lightweight modular unit which installs anywhere without floor reinforcement or other structural change.

Unheated, oxygen rich air from outside is brought in to support combustion. Thus precious heated house air is preserved. In addition a simple lever connected to an internal damper permits you to control the amount of combustion air supplied to the firebox. You can actually turn the Lighthouse "up" or "down," much as you would a gas flame.

A self-contained heat exchanger removes thermal energy from the hot combustion gases on their way to the chimney or flue. Normal interior house air is taken from the cool air return of the home's existing duct work, forced over the heat exchanger, and returned to the hot air return of the home's duct work to be distributed throughout the house by the existing forced air furnace fan. The Lighthouse plenum contains an electrical resistor that turns the furnace fan on and off as needed.

U/L approved, and weighing only 390 pounds fully assembled, the Lighthouse can be installed flush to a wall, partly recessed in the wall, or extending through the wall to provide fireplace beauty to two rooms.

No special insulation nor floor reinforcement is required. So the Lighthouse can be installed either professionally or as a do-it-yourself project.

Fireplaces can also be free-standing units, needing only a special flue and fire-protective surround material.

It looks like brick…

…but is cheaper and faster to use. WonderBrix has many of the advantages of brick--it is fireproof and easy to keep looking good--but is actually a compound that you can trowel on over prearranged squares of tape. You pull the tapes off and the material hardens into the look and feel of real brick. The tapes use color codes to make sure the bricks are consistent in size and pattern.

Tape can be applied to a clean stucco surface (or cement block wall) without prior treatment. For any other surface a white coating is first applied by brush or roller to give the mortarlike appearance between bricks.

One advantage of Wonderbrix around fireplaces is that it is fireproof, so that you do not need to leave a safety clearance. It can also be extended in front of the fireplace to give the impression of a brick hearth.

Apply side marker strips from the roll along the left and right edge of the area to be covered. Start the strips with the top edge of a "black mark" at the ceiling; run the strips down the wall to the floor. (If you want the bricks to be flush to ceiling, start the strips at bottom edge of a "black mark.")

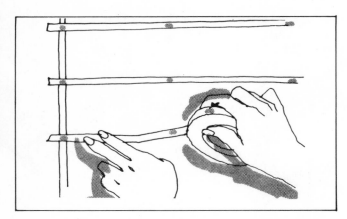

Start with either a "red mark" or a "green mark" (it doesn't matter which, as long as you start them all the same), apply pattern strips horizontally across the wall. Begin horizontal strips at every "black mark" found on the vertical side strips, starting at top of wall and working down.

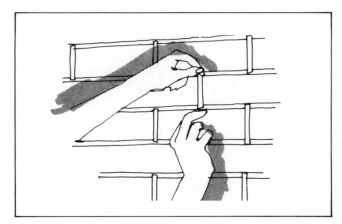

To create brick pattern, use perforated sections, alternating their position on each course. First row would take red mark to red mark; second row would take green mark to green mark, etc., for a staggered brick design.

This fireplace accent wall has been covered using three types of Wonderbrix
materials--stucco, stone template and coloring, and brick. Each requires a different arrangement, but employs the same thick troweled-on material. The arched and vertical
brick designs are made with the usual tape system, but with a different pattern, as described in the owner's-use manual.

Supply and Information Sources

Basic materials for remodeling your living room—lumber, plywood, plasterboard, concrete, paneling, nails, etc.—will be available locally at hardware, paint and lumber outlets or at home centers that are a combination kind of store with all kinds of supplies for remodeling. Wood parquet flooring, vinyl tile and sheet flooring, ceiling tile and various wallcoverings also will be sold in these centers.

For some special kinds of furniture lumber, veneers and special hardware and fancy moldings, you'll have to buy from a mail-order source that sells to home craftspersons and cabinetmakers. These sources are listed, and your best bet is to send for their catalogs, then make a selection from the many items that are shown in the catalogs.

The addresses of companies that provided photographs are listed, and if you contact them they will send you the names and addresses of dealers near you. Most companies will send colorful brochures, and most are constantly introducing new products, so it's possible you'll learn about new items even before your local dealers stocks them.

Companies and Associations Listed In The Text

American Olean Tile, Lansdale, PA 19446

American Plywood Association, 1119 A St., Tacoma, WA 98401

Armstrong Cork Company, Lancaster, PA 17604

Azrock Floor Products, P.O. Box 531, San Antonio, TX 78292

Baseway™ Strips from Carlon, Three Commerce Park Square, 23200 Chagrin Blvd., P.O. Box 22310, Cleveland, OH 44122

Birge Wallpaper, 2665 Broadway, Cheektowago, NY 14225

Boise Cascade, Box 514, Berryville, VA 22611

California Redwood Association, 617 Montgomery St., San Francisco, CA 94111

Elmer's Adhesive, Borden Chemical Co., 180 E. Broad St., Columbus, OH 43215

Fireplace Institute, 111 E. Wacker Drive, Chicago, IL 60601

Forest Fiber Products, P.O. Box 68, Forest Grove, OR 97116

Heatilator Brand Fireplace, Div. Vega Industries, Inc., Mt. Pleasant, IA 52641

Marlite Div., Masonite Corporation, Dover, OH 44622

Masonite Corporation, 29 N. Wacker Drive, Chicago, IL 60606

NuTone Div., Scovil, Madison & Red Bank Roads, Cincinnati, OH 45227

Pope and Talbot, P.O. Box 8171, 1700 S.W. Fourth Ave., Portland, OR 97207

Rollerwall, Inc. (formerly Designer Paint Supply Co.), P.O. Box 757, Silver Springs, MD 20901

Roxite Div., Masonite Coroporation, 7800 N. Milwaukee Avenue, Nile, IL 60648

Stanley Tool Works, New Britain, Conn. 06050

Superior Fireplace, 4325 Artesia Avenue, Fullerton, CA 92633

Thermograte Enterprises, Inc., 51 Iona Lane, St. Paul, MN 55117

Thomas Industries, Residential Lighting Div., 207 E. Broadway, Louisville, KY 40202

Western Wood Products Association, 1500 Yeon Bldg., Portland, OR 97204

Wing Sales Company, 918 E. Cedar Lane, Payson, AZ 85541

Wonder Brix, 222 Wisconsin Bldg., Lake Forest, ILL. 60045

Z-Brick Company, Woodinville, WA 98072

Furniture-Grade Hardwoods, Specialty Hardware, Etc.

Albert Constantine and Son, 2050 Eastchester Road, Bronx, NY 10461

Craftsman Wood Service, 2727 S. Mary Street, Chicago, IL 60608

Educational Lumber Co., P.O. Box 5373, Asheville, NC 28803

Minnesota Woodworkers Supply Co., Rogers, MN 55374

Windows, Including Bays, Sliding Glass Doors, with Insulating Glass

Andersen Windowall®, Bayport, MN 55003

R.O.W. Window Sales, 1365 Academy Ave., Ferndale, MI 48220

Rolscreen Company, Pella, IA 50219

Index

Other SUCCESSFUL Books

SUCCESSFUL SPACE SAVING AT HOME. The conquest of inner space in apartments, whether tiny or ample, and homes, inside and out. Storage and built-in possibilities for all living areas, with a special section of illustrated tips from the professional space planners. 8½"x11"; 128 pp; over 150 B-W and color photographs and illustrations. $12.00 Cloth. $4.95 Paper.

BOOK OF SUCCESSFUL HOME PLANS. Published in cooperation with Home Planners, Inc.; designs by Richard B. Pollman. A collection of 226 outstanding home plans, plus information on standards and clearances as outlined in HUD's *Manual of Acceptable Practices.* 8½"x11"; 192 pp; over 500 illustrations. $12.00 Cloth. $4.95 Paper.

HOW TO CUT YOU ENERGY BILLS, Derven and Nichols. A homeowner's guide designed not for just the fix-it person, but for everyone. Instructions on how to save money and fuel in all areas—lighting, appliances, insulation, caulking, and much more. If it's on your utility bill, you'll find it here. 8½"x11"; 136 pp; over 200 photographs and illustrations. $12.00 Cloth. $4.95 Paper.

FINDING & FIXING THE OLDER HOME, Schram. Tells how to check for tell-tale signs of damage when looking for homes and how to appraise and finance them. Points out the particular problems found in older homes, with instructions on how to remedy them. 8½"x11"; 160 pp; over 200 photographs and illustrations. $12.00 Cloth. $4.95 Paper.

WALL COVERINGS AND DECORATION, Banov. Describes and evaluates different types of papers, fabrics, foils and vinyls, and paneling. Chapters on art selection, principles of design and color. Complete installation instructions for all materials. 8½"x11"; 136 pp; over 150 B-W and color photographs and illustrations. $12.00 Cloth. $4.95 Paper.

BOOK OF SUCCESSFUL PAINTING, Banov. Everything about painting any surface, inside or outside. Includes surface preparation, paint selection and application, problems, and color in decorating. "Before dipping brush into paint, a few hours spent with this authoritative guide could head off disaster." —*Publishers Weekly.* 8½"x11"; 114 pp; over 150 B-W and color photographs and illustrations. $12.00 Cloth. $4.95 Paper.

BOOK OF SUCCESSFUL BATHROOMS, Schram. Complete guide to remodeling or decorating a bathroom to suit individual needs and tastes. Materials are recommended that have more than one function, need no periodic refinishing, and fit into different budgets. Complete installation instructions. 8½"x11"; 128 pp; over 200 B-W and color photographs. (Chosen by Interior Design, Woman's How-to, and Popular Science Book Clubs) $12.00 Cloth. $4.95 Paper.

TOTAL HOME PROTECTION, Miller. How to make your home burglarproof, fireproof, accidentproof, termiteproof, windproof, and lightningproof. With specific instructions and product recommendations. 8½"x11"; 124 pp; over 150 photographs and illustrations. (Chosen by McGraw-Hill's Architects Book Club) $12.00 Cloth. $4.95 Paper.

BOOK OF SUCCESSFUL SWIMMING POOLS, Derven and Nichols. Everything the present or would-be pool owner should know, from what kind of pool he can afford and site location, to construction, energy savings, accessories and maintenance and safety. 8½"x11"; over 250 B-W and color photographs and illustrations; 128 pp. $12.00 Cloth. $4.95 Paper.

HOW TO BUILD YOUR OWN HOME, Reschke. Construction methods and instructions for wood-frame ranch, one-and-a-half story, two-story, and split level homes, with specific recommendations for materials and products. 8½"x11"; 336 pages; over 600 photographs, illustrations, and charts. (Main selection for McGraw-Hill's Engineers Book Club) $14.00 Cloth. $5.95 Paper.

SUCCESSFUL STUDIOS AND WORK CENTERS Davidson. How and where to set up work centers at home for the professional or amateur—for art projects, photography, sewing, woodworking, pottery and jewelry, or home office work. The author covers equipment, floor plans, basic light/plumbing/wiring requirements, and adds interviews with artists, photographers, and other professionals telling how they handled space and work problems. 8½"x11"; 144 pp; over 200 photographs and diagrams. $12.00 Cloth. $4.95 Paper.

SUCCESSFUL FAMILY AND RECREATION ROOMS, Cornell. How to best use already finished rooms or convert spaces such as garage, basement, or attic into family/recreation rooms. Along with basics like lighting, ventilation, plumbing, and traffic patterns, the author discusses "mood setters" (color schemes, fireplaces, bars, etc.) and finishing details (flooring, wall covering, ceilings, built-ins, etc.) A special chapter gives quick ideas for problem areas. 8½"x11"; 144 pp; over 250 photos and diagrams. (Featured alternate for McGraw-Hill Book Clubs.) $12.00 Cloth. $4.95 Paper.

SUCCESSFUL HOME GREENHOUSES, Scheller. Instructions, complete with diagrams, for building all types of greenhouses. Among topics covered are: site location, climate control, drainage, ventilation, use of sun, auxiliary equipment, and maintenance. Charts provide characteristics and requirements of plants and greenhouse layouts are included in appendices. "One of the most completely detailed volumes of advice for those contemplating an investment in a greenhouse." *Publishers Weekly.* 8½"x11"; 136 pp; over 200 photos and diagrams. (Featured alternates of the Popular Science and McGraw-Hill Book Clubs). $12.00 Cloth. $4.95 Paper.

BOOK OF SUCCESSFUL FIREPLACES, 20th ed., Lytle. The expanded, updated edition of the book that has been a standard of the trade for over 50 years—over a million copies sold! Advice is given on selecting from the many types of fireplaces available, on planning and adding fireplaces, on building fires, on constructing and using barbecues. Also includes new material on wood as a fuel, woodburning stoves, and energy savings. 8½"x11"; 128 pp; over 250 photos and illustrations. $12.00 Cloth. $5.95 Paper.

SUCCESSFUL ROOFING & SIDING, Reschke. "This well-illustrated and well-organized book offers many practical ideas for improving a home's exterior." *Library Journal.* Here is full information about dealing with contractors, plus instructions specific enough for the do-it-yourselfer. All topics—from carrying out a structural checkup to supplemental exterior work like dormers, insulation, and gutters,—are fully covered. Materials to suit all budgets and home styles are reviewed and evaluated. 8½"x11"; 160 pp; over 300 photos and illustrations. $12.00 Cloth. $5.95 Paper. (Main selection Popular Science and McGraw-Hill Book Clubs)

PRACTICAL & DECORATIVE CONCRETE, Wilde. "Spells it all out for you... is good for beginner or talented amateur... What this book does is inspire you to try the fancy stuff." *Detroit Sunday News.* Complete information for the layman on the use of concrete inside or outside the home. The author—Executive Director of the American Concrete Institute—gives instructions for the installation, maintenance, and repair of foundations, walkways, driveways, steps, embankments, fences, tree wells, patios, and also suggests "fun" projects. 8½"x11"; 144 pp; over 150 photos and illustrations. $12.00 Cloth. $4.95 Paper. (Featured alternate, Popular Science and McGraw-Hill Book Clubs)

SUCCESSFUL PET HOMES, Mueller. "There are years worth of projects...The text is good and concise—all around, I am most impressed." *Roger Caras, Pets and Wildlife, CBS.* "A thoroughly delightful and helpful book for everyone who loves animals." *Syndicated reviewer, Lisa Oglesby.* Here is a new approach to keeping both pet owners and pets happy by choosing, buying, building functional but inexpensive houses, carriers, feeders, and play structures for dogs, cats, and birds. The concerned pet owner will find useful advice on providing for pet needs with the least wear and tear on the home. 8½"x11"; 116 pp; over 200 photos and illustrations. Cloth $12.00. $4.95 Paper.

SUCCESSFUL HOME ADDITIONS, Schram. For homeowners who want more room but would like to avoid the inconvenience and distress of moving, three types of home additions are discussed: garage conversion with carport added; bedroom, bathroom, sauna addition; major home renovation which includes the addition of a second-story master suite and family room. All these remodeling projects have been successfully completed and, from them, step-by-step coverage has been reported of almost all potential operations in adding on to a home. The straightforward presentation of information on materials, methods, and costs, as well as a glossary of terms, enables the homeowner to plan, arrange contracting, or take on some of the work personally in order to cut expenses. 8½"x11"; 144 pp; over 300 photos and illustrations. Cloth $12.00. Paper $5.95.

SUCCESSFUL PLANTERS, Orcutt. Build a planter, and use it for a room divider, a living wall, a kitchen herb garden, a centerpiece, a table, an aquarium—and don't settle for anything that looks homemade! The plans and instructions provided here give not only a functional finished product, but a professional-looking one. Along with construction steps, there is advice on the best types of planters for individual plants, how to locate them for best sun and shade, and how to provide the best care to keep plants healthy and beautiful, inside or outside the home. 8½x11"; 136 pp; over 200 photos and illustrations. Cloth $12.00. Paper $4.95.

FINISHING OFF, Galvin. A book for both the new-home owner buying a "bonus space" house, and those who want to make use of previously unused areas of their homes. The author advises which jobs can be handled by the homeowner, and which should be contracted out. Projects include: putting in partitions and doors to create rooms; finishing off floors and walls and ceilings; converting attics and basements; designing kitchens and bathrooms, and installing fixtures and cabinets. Information is given for materials that best suit each job, with specifics on tools, costs, and building procedures. 8½x11"; 144 pp; over 250 photos and illustrations. Cloth $12.00. Paper $5.95.

Structures Publishing Company   Box 423   *Farmington, Michigan 48024*